MAY – 9 2014

INSIGHT GUIDES

EXPLORE
BALI

WITHDRAWN

CONTENTS

Introduction

Recommended Routes for... 4
Explore Bali 8
Food and Drink 14
Shopping 18
Entertainment 20
Activities 22
History: Key Dates 24

Directory

Accommodation 84
Restaurants 94
Nightlife 104
A–Z 106
Language 118
Books and Film 120

Credits

About This Book 122
Credits 123
Index 124

Best Routes

1. Sanur, Denpasar and Uluwatu 28
2. Ubud Highlights 35
3. Batur and Kintamani 42
4. Bedulu, Tampaksiring and Tegallalang 45
5. Pejeng and Bangli 50
6. Klungkung and Besakih 53
7. Tenganan, Candidasa and Amlapura 56
8. Bratan and Bedugul 61
9. Lovina and Singaraja 66
10. Krambitan, Pupuan and Medewi 70
11. Tanah Lot, Jatiluwih and Batukau 73
12. Nusa Lembongan, Nusa Ceningan and Nusa Penida 77

ARCHITECTURE

View the ceremonial longhouses of Tenganan (route 7), the 'Mother Temple' of Besakih (route 6), the water palace of Taman Ujung (route 7) and the Brahma Arama Vihara (route 9).

RECOMMENDED ROUTES FOR...

ART FANS

Marvel at the artwork in the museums of Ubud (route 2), a Belgian artist's museum-home in Sanur (route 1) and the fabulous painted ceilings of the Kerta Gosa at Klungkung (route 6).

BEACH LOVERS

Sea and sun worshippers will appreciate the white sands of Nusa Lembongan (route 12) and the dark sand bay of Lovina (route 9).

CULTURE SEEKERS

Choose from the monuments of Denpasar (route 1), the museums of Ubud (route 2), the royal history of Klungkung (route 6), the temple of Tanah Lot (route 11) and Pejeng and Bangli (route 5).

FAMILIES

Swing through the trees like Tarzan at Bali Treetop Adventure Park (route 8), ride elephants at the Elephant Safari Park (route 4) and witness glorious culture at Tenganan (route 7).

FLORA AND FAUNA

Bali's beautiful nature is a big draw for visitors; you can observe monkeys and herons (route 2), elephants, dolphins, the wildlife of West Bali National Park (route 9) and the magnificent flora of Gunung Batukau (route 11).

SPORTS ENTHUSIASTS

Dive and snorkel amongst the marine life in Candidasa and Amed. Get your water sports fix at Lake Bratan (route 8) and Nusa Lembongan (route 12), or surf the challenging waves of Uluwatu (route 1) and Medewi (route 10).

VIEWFINDERS

Be blown away by Batur and Kintamani (route 3), Bedulu, Tampaksiring and Tegallalang (route 4), Bangli (route 5), West Bali National Park (route 9), Pupuan (route 10) and Gunung Batukau (route 11).

INTRODUCTION

An introduction to Bali's geography, customs and culture, plus illuminating background information on cuisine, history and what to do when you're there.

Explore Bali	8
Food and Drink	14
Shopping	18
Entertainment	20
Activities	22
History: Key Dates	24

3 0053 01126 0190

Flowers at Candikuning

EXPLORE BALI

Bali is often described using travel writing clichés: exotic, seductive, magical. Although these words lose their power through overuse, they still best describe the island's charms – anything less seems inadequate.

For a tiny island in the world's largest archipelago, Bali has an astonishing diversity. The international airport is located in the southern region of Badung, the urban and commercial centre of Bali. This is where most visitors play and party all day long and late into the night, mostly in the beach towns of Kuta, Legian and Seminyak. The more sedate Sanur and Nusa Dua areas allow for more self-contained hedonism. Yet south Bali is not without redemption, for behind the blatant

Straw boxes for temple offerings

commercialisation are some of the island's most traditional aspects. In the regions of Gianyar and Bangli, the contours become softer, the villages smaller and the culture more unfettered. Bali's earliest kingdoms carved out realms in these fertile lands and left behind a legacy of ancient temples. Ubud especially is a magnet for culture, with many of its surrounding villages specialising in particular arts, crafts, dances or musical styles.

Eastward in the regions of Klungkung and Karangasem are areas of striking contrasts, dominated by the island's highest mountain Gunung (Mt) Agung, the spiritual focus for most Balinese. Isolated villages, still conservative by nature, continue to maintain artistic traditions and ancient customs. The northern coast of Bali, the region of Buleleng, is mainly agricultural, growing everything from spices to grapes. Mountains almost meet the sea on narrow black sand beaches washed by calm waves.

Western Bali, the region of Jembrana and part of Buleleng, is a mix of dry and lush, and ignored by most travellers. Sparsely populated yet cultur-

Temple festival (odilan)

Puru Ulun Danu Bratan

ally diverse, a national park with rare wildlife anchors this part of the island. Finally, the southwest Tabanan region is the rice basket of Bali, once home to powerful royal dynasties and today, rural villages scattered on sloping plains watered by crater lakes nestled under hulking volcanoes.

A chain of six volcanoes, ranging in height between 1,350m (4,400ft) and 3,014m (9,800ft) above sea level, stretches from the west to the east of Bali. The beaches in the south consist of white sand, while beaches in other parts of the island are of dark volcanic sand.

BALI TOURS

Bali has an area of 5,632 sq km (2,175 sq miles), measuring just 90km (55 miles) along the north-south axis and 140km (87 miles) from east to west. The island's compact size means that most of the island can be explored through scenic drives and walks, very often on day trips.

The 12 routes in this book cover most of the island's main sights, and, with the exception of the Lovina and Singaraja trip (route 9), are all suitable for visitors based in the south or in Ubud, and designed as single-day trips. Visitors who are not restricted to one specific base can, however, link some of the routes and use them as a guide for exploring larger areas of the island – we have suggested possible

links in the grey fact boxes at the start of each route.

With the exception of the Nusa Lembongan route (No. 12), all itineraries are road trips. We recommend that you arrange for a car and driver, so that you can relax and enjoy the scenery – driving in Bali can be dangerous, and road signs can be confusing or inadequate (see page 116). Traffic jams are common, especially at rush hour in the built-up areas in the south. Note that Denpasar (route 1), in particular, is not an easy city to navigate by car due to a complexity of one-way streets and the lack of parking space.

TOURISM

Since the 1960s Bali has been defined and propelled forwards by tourism. Although some anthropologists charge that this has resulted in the loss of Balinese innocence and a commercialisation of its traditional culture, it is clear that tourism has been the making of Bali over the past few decades. In the island's arts and crafts industry and in the performing arts at least, there can be no doubt of tourism's revitalising effects. Today, thousands of villagers produce craft items both for the local tourism market and for export. Traditional village architects rebuild temples using time-honoured principles, while their university-trained counterparts design luxury hotels incorporating Balinese

Pura Gunung Kawi, Tampaksiring

elements. All of these efforts are part of a creative process that has been going on for centuries in Bali: the resilience of Balinese culture comes from its remarkable ability to adopt, adapt and absorb.

CLIMATE

Bali has a tropical climate appropriate to its proximity eight degrees south of the equator. Year-round temperatures average 30°C (86°F). High humidity can be expected during the rainy season between mid-October and mid-April, while humidity is lowest during the dry season, from May to September. The rainy season brings daily downpours, dramatic thunderstorms and overcast days, with the greatest rainfall recorded between December and February. From June to August there is a very refreshing cool breeze, and you can expect constant sunshine. The mountainous regions offer a cooler alternative, especially at night.

POPULATION

Bali has a population of 3.9 million, of which the overwhelming majority is Hindu (noteworthy, given that Indonesia is the world's most populous Muslim nation). There are, however, a few pockets of long-established Muslims, Christians and Buddhists residing in rural areas; people who are usually descendants of enduring populations, with origins elsewhere in the Indonesian-Malaysian region. These people, whose histories in Bali stretch far back, have adopted the Balinese identity and are culturally Balinese.

There is also a growing number of Muslim and Christian immigrants from neighbouring islands who come in search of jobs. The new arrivals have settled mainly in the urban areas of southern Bali, where they serve as a cheap labour force. Most people, especially the young, live in the capital city and administrative centre of Denpasar, as well as the tourist areas on the south coast, and the inland town of Ubud.

Balinese people speak Indonesian, but generally revert to Balinese in their homes. English is widely spoken in all the tourist areas, but often not understood in the more remote villages and farming communities. For more information on local languages, see page 112. For useful vocabulary, see page 118.

LOCAL CUSTOMS

There are four types of holiday in Indonesia: religious, national, international and commemorative. Ones that are designated *tanggal merah* (literally red date, or designated in red on a calendar) signify national holidays, when government offices, schools and banks are closed. However, the majority of shops, restaurants, travel agents and tourist attractions in Bali remain open on these days. Many of the dates of religious holidays vary from year to year.

Legong dancers

Exotic fruit

If you are visiting Bali in March or April, you may be there for Nyepi (Balinese New Year), which occurs on the day following the dark moon of the spring equinox. This is when the island retreats into silence for 24 hours. On this darkest of nights the Balinese will not cook, work or travel, there are no flights into or out of Bali, shops remain closed, all streets are deserted and no lights are switched on.

DON'T LEAVE BALI WITHOUT...

Visiting a market. Food markets, characterised by strong aromas and lots of hustle and bustle, can be found all over the island. From as early as 4am, a bounty of fruit and vegetables including cauliflowers, avocados, bananas, pineapples, lemongrass, chillies, peanuts, shallots, mangosteen, rambutan and *salak* (snakefruit), is off-loaded from trucks and artistically arranged by the vendors. See page 61.

Watching the sunset at Petulu. Every evening thousands of white Javan pond herons and plumed egrets return to roost in the trees. The herons are said to be a manifestation of the human soul. See page 40.

Catching a Balinese dance. The *legong* is performed by three young girls: two principal dancers and an attendant. The usual version is the tale of a king and the princess he has abducted, with the performers exquisitely dressed. The *kecak* dance involves up to 150 men in sarongs crouching in concentric circles around a flickering lamp and chanting hypnotically while the story is acted out in the circle. Inspired by a 1920s ritual trance-dance called *sanghyang*, it is taken from the Hindu epic *Ramayana*. See page 20.

Kicking back on the island of Nusa Lembongan. The white-sand beaches at Jungutbatu and Mushroom Bay along the island's western coast are ringed with cosy guesthouses and boutique resorts, while beach clubs offer snorkelling and diving facilities for day trippers arriving on catamarans. As well as the famous diving opportunities, there is a lively surf scene along the south coast at Dream Beach. See page 77.

Gazing at the awesome rice terraces of Jatiluwih. This area of central Bali presents a landscape of endless sculpted rice terraces against a mountain backdrop. Jatiluwih has been a Unesco World Heritage Site since 2008 for its preservation of traditional Balinese farming techniques. Jatiluwih means 'extraordinary' which is an apt description for this spellbinding vista. See page 75.

Seeing the ancient site of Gunung Kawi. This amazing complex of rock-hewn *candi* (shrines) facades and monks' alcoves nestles in a scenic valley overlooking the Pakerisan River. Dating back to the 11th century, the carvings are remarkably preserved royal memorials for members of Bali's Warmadewa dynasty. Next to the main group of five *candi* across the river are a cluster of niches and rooms hacked out of the rock. See page 47.

Air Panas hot springs

POLITICS

Bali is one of the 26 provinces of Indonesia, whose president, Susilo Bambang Yudhoyono (SBY), is the chief of state, head of government and supreme commander-in-chief of the armed forces. The next presidential election will be held in mid-2014. After decades under a dictatorship, Indonesia has evolved in the past decade into a democracy. While the country is predominantly Muslim, the government is secular, with a constitutional obligation to protect religious freedom. The Indonesian government officially recognises five religions: Islam, Protestantism, Catholicism, Buddhism and Hinduism.

ECONOMY

In addition to revenue from tourism, Bali's economy is sustained by the export of artisanal goods and agricultural products. The chain of mountains dividing the island is responsible for the different climatic conditions and soil types, so Bali produces a huge variety of crops. The southern-central plains are extensively cultivated – the landscape is dominated by terraced rice fields, but heading inland these become gardens of onions, cabbages and papayas, and in the higher regions coffee, tobacco, cloves, chillies, oranges and peanuts, all of which thrive in the cooler climate.

The farmers who live in the rain shadow of the mountain range, in the hot northern-coastal region, cultivate dry-land crops such as maize, cassava, beans and grapes. Fishing and seaweed farming are also important commodities for foreign markets.

It is this contrast of agricultural activities and artistic endeavour, combined with dramatic scenery and a culture long associated with grace and hospitality, that makes Bali such an appealing place to visit.

Balinese Hindu culture

Religion is still the central spine of the Balinese way of life and philosophy, with the temple, or *pura*, the focus of every Hindu community on the island. When it is a matter of tradition and spiritual duty, even the young generation swaps its jeans and business suits for a sarong and heads to the temple or to one of the many village events – from a birth celebration, tooth-filing ceremony (to be rid of evil), wedding or cremation. Any visitor who spends more than a few days on the island is certain to witness some kind of temple festival, colourful procession, or ceremony. The *odilan*, or temple anniversary celebration, is a particularly lavish occasion in Bali. As the date varies from one temple to another, you may well have the opportunity to catch one during your visit.

Rice terraces   *Outrigger boats at Amed*

Opening times. Shopping malls are generally open daily from 9 or 10am until 10 or 11pm, while the shops in Kuta and Seminyak are open from 9am until 9pm. Smaller shops and wholesale outlets (such as the shops in Tegallalang) will close at 5pm and are closed on Sundays.

Seafood feast. The Jimbaran seafood feast is synonymous with holidays in Bali. Beaches are typically lined with cafés serving that day's fishy catch. As you watch the sun set over the sea, barbecued fish, giant prawns, lobster, squid and clams, accompanied by rice, the Balinese water spinach known as *kangkung*, and homemade Balinese sauces, will be brought to your table.

Daluman drink. The daluman stall in Ubud's market serves a thick jelly-like drink formed from the health-giving leaves of the daluman vine. Apparently, it's full of vitamins and good for pregnant women; it tastes quite good, although the slimy texture can take some getting used to.

Water sports off Candidasa. There are several superb snorkelling and dive sites off both Candidasa and Amed. Ask at any of the hotels in Candidasa, where you can arrange to be taken in a traditional *jukung* fishing boat to Tepekong Island and the tiny Mimpang Islands, where there are several coral walls. In Amed, there are several scuba diving companies, or you can swim out and snorkel around a small Japanese shipwreck off Banyuning Beach. You will see a variety of marine life, including corals, nudibranch and psychedelic fish. In the open waters you may even spot sharks and manta rays.

Pasir Putih Beach. The most beautiful beach on the coastline is Pasir Putih, meaning 'white sands', situated 6km (4 miles) east of Candidasa. Fringed by a coconut grove and flanked by green headlands with a sheer cliff behind, it is accessed by a 600m/yd track, which, although rough and steep, is negotiable by car. The tranquil ambience and the peppering of simple grass-roofed *warungs* (cafés) are reminiscent of Bali in the 1970s.

Rainforest trek. You can trek through the rainforest between Lake Buyan and Lake Tamblingan, an area abundant in birdlife, where you may spot babblers, woodpeckers, ground thrushes and malkohas. On the road above this shoulder of land is a temple and a sign to Pura Ulun Danu Tamblingan, directing you 400m/yds down a meandering flight of steps to another temple beside the lake's edge; this one has a multi-roofed *meru* (pagoda).

Oceanic sunfish. The channel between Nusa Lembongan and Nusa Penida is a renowned breeding ground for the Mola mola, or oceanic sunfish, a large flattened fish with elongated dorsal and ventral fins. It is the world's heaviest-known bony fish, with an average adult weight of 1,000kg (2,200lb). It attracts divers from around the world and can be spotted from July to November.

Preparing babi guling at Gianyar market

FOOD AND DRINK

The island caters for every taste, from street-food served out of boxes balanced on bicycles and prepared at the road side, to gourmet cuisine presented in world-class restaurants.

The exciting news for epicures is that both local and international restaurants can be found in abundance in Bali's tourist areas, with a huge range of styles, settings and cuisines. The mouth-watering creations of Bali's five-star chefs are testament to the quality and diversity of the fresh produce of this fertile island; by creating a demand for premium fruit and vegetables (including organic produce), suppliers, retailers, restaurateurs and hoteliers are not only supporting the local farmers, but showcasing Bali's bountiful harvest.

noodles); *sate* served with a sweet and spicy peanut sauce; *cap cay*, consisting of wok-tossed seasonal vegetables; and *gado-gado*, a warm salad of blanched, mixed vegetables, tofu and hard-boiled egg served with peanut sauce.

Staple Balinese fare

In everyday Balinese cooking, prepared by the women and eaten at home as well as at *warungs* (small road-side stalls), the staple ingredient is rice, eaten with small portions of spicy vegetables, fish, meat and eggs, and accompanied by *sambal*

LOCAL CUISINE

Beware the fiery chillies

Indonesian cuisine

Indonesian cuisine varies greatly by region. Many speciality dishes were influenced by the early Arabic, Chinese, Indian and Dutch traders and settlers. Local curries incorporate freshly ground spices and seasonings such as lemongrass, ginger, kaffir lime leaves and tamarind. Simple Indonesian dishes include *nasi campur*, comprised of rice and a selection of vegetables, meat or fish, egg and other accompaniments; *nasi goreng* (fried rice); *mie goreng* (fried

Roadside fruit for sale

(hot paste ground from fiery chillies). This type of dish, again known as *nasi campur*, is usually cooked in the early morning and consumed whenever hunger hits. Another popular way of cooking is to wrap minced and highly seasoned meat, fish or poultry in banana-leaf parcels and steam them, or set the parcels directly onto hot coals to roast. Known as *tum*, these banana-leaf packets are served in most Balinese homes. *Pepes ikan*, where minced spiced fish is the filling, is a favourite delicacy as the banana leaf seals in the juices.

Balinese cooking favours the use of coconuts (either grated or as coconut milk), peanuts (which are ground into a paste to form a sweet and spicy sauce), and salted and fermented shrimp paste, used to enliven dishes. *Tempe*, a nutty slab made from fermented soy beans, is a delicious and inexpensive source of protein. Fresh spices, garlic, onions and hot fresh chillies are also used in abundance, meaning that dishes – while deliciously fragrant – can also be tantalisingly hot.

Balinese – and Indonesian – desserts include *bubuh injin*, which is a sweet and sticky black rice pudding, named after the colour of the rice husk and served with coconut milk sauce. *Pisang goreng* is banana fried in batter and served with syrup, while *kue dadar* are little crêpe parcels filled with palm sugar, vanilla and grated coconut. Other favourites include sweets, jellies, tapioca and sticky cakes, generally garnished with grated coconut and presented in shades of pink and green.

Festive dishes

In contrast to everyday dishes, which are prepared by women, special ceremonial food is prepared in an elaborate manner by men, and then eaten communally. The dishes, which can be ordered in advance at some restaurants, include *babi guling* (a slow-cooked spit-roasted pig stuffed with onion, garlic, peppercorns and herbs, and brushed with crushed turmeric), *bebek betutu* (duck stuffed with spices, wrapped in banana leaves and smoked overnight in an earth-oven), *lawar* (spicy raw meat mashed with grated coconut and blood) and *sate lilit* (satay of spiced, minced meat or fish with an infusion of coconut, pressed onto a lemongrass skewer).

WHERE TO EAT

In Seminyak, Kuta, Sanur, Ubud and Nusa Dua and the surrounding areas, there are restaurants serving upmarket international cuisine from Italy, Greece, France, Belgium, Spain, Mexico, India, Morocco, China, Japan, Korea, Thailand and more, as well as local specialities from Bali and across the Indonesian archipelago. Simple speciality restaurants from Sumatra, Java, Sulawesi and other Indonesian islands are to be found mainly in the south of Bali, particularly in Denpasar and parts of Kuta and Seminyak. Outside the tourist areas you will

Beautifully presented sushi at Ku De Ta

find small *warungs* (cafés) serving simple Indonesian dishes. Five-star resorts typically have superb restaurants and world-class chefs. Many restaurants also have their own bakeries on the premises, serving delicious breads, pastries and cakes.

For the visitor, genuine Balinese cuisine (as opposed to Indonesian or Indonesian-Chinese food) can be difficult to find. But if you search hard enough, you can track down truly local dishes at some market stalls (especially on main market days), at some *warungs* and at the handful of restaurants now aware that visitors want to try authentic Balinese cuisine.

Seminyak

Seminyak's fashionable 'Eat Street' stretches from Jl Kayu Aya (also known as Jl Laksmana and Oberoi St) through Jl Petitenget, and if you were to eat out there every night, it would take weeks to appraise every restaurant on this strip. There is something to suit all budgets, and competition means that standards remain high.

As you walk through the doors of some of these restaurants, you may be excused for believing that you have been transported to anywhere but Bali – from a Greek island, to a Moroccan kasbah, to a Japanese *izakaya*. A number of restaurants offer alfresco dining in fabulous locations overlooking the Indian Ocean.

Indonesian rijsttafel

Rijsttafel, literally meaning 'rice-table' and originating from the Dutch plantation owners, is a great way to selectively sample the Indonesian cuisine. It is easy to find, presented as a buffet at most of the middle-market and upmarket tourist hotels as well as at restaurants that cater for large numbers. The elaborate meal includes an assortment of meat, seafood and vegetable dishes, salads, spring rolls and *sate*, accompanied by rice crackers and a collection of pickles, spicy *sambals* (optional condiments in consideration of personal palates) and sauces, and followed by local desserts and fresh fruits. The objective is to feature not only an array of multi-textured specialities, but also flavours, colours and degrees of spiciness. The Balinese version is called *megibung* and will combine local delicacies with Balinese *bumbu* – a spice paste that varies from village to village.

Rijsttafel buffet

Trattoria-style restaurant

Lobster dumplings

LOCAL DRINKS

Beer

The bestselling brand of beer in Bali is Bintang, produced by Multi Bintang Indonesia, an Indonesian subsidiary of Heineken. This 5 percent pilsner (clear, bottom-fermented lager beer) is delightfully refreshing when served ice-cold. It is readily available from bars, restaurants, supermarkets and convenience stores, but may be a little harder to find outside the tourist areas or in Muslim-owned stores and eateries.

Tuak, arak and brem

Other local brews include *tuak* (palm-beer, strange-tasting and intoxicating), and *arak*, the local firewater, made from palm sap and drunk neat or with a sweet mixer. Be warned that *arak* has an unrefined character and there have recently been a number of deaths among tourists and locals alike due to tainting with methanol. You are strongly advised not to drink *arak*-based cocktails or locally produced spirits. Brem Bali, a sweet rice wine, is another popular, traditional drink, made from sticky white rice known as *ketan*, with a smaller amount of *injin*, Indonesian black rice. Besides being a beverage, it is a requirement for many Hindu ceremonies.

Balinese wine

Surprisingly, grapes have been cultivated in the hot and arid northern coastal region of the island since the beginning of the 20th century. It was only a few decades ago, however, that grapes were grown satisfactorily on a large scale and marketed throughout the Indonesian archipelago. This led to the creation of an industry that is not traditionally associated with Bali, and 1994 saw the establishment of Hatten Wines. The company now produces eight different all-Balinese wines, which are natural and free of colouring, flavouring and concentrates.

While imported spirits and fine wines from around the world are available in Bali, the selection is often limited and prices are excessive due to the application of high customs and excise tax.

Fresh fruit juices

Bali is famous for its fresh fruit and vegetable juices, including pineapple, avocado laced with chocolate, or innovative blends such as passionfruit, watermelon and papaya. Meanwhile, the fresh young coconut drink known as *kelapa muda* is either sipped straight from the shell or served with ice and supplemented by slithers of slippery young coconut flesh.

Food and Drink Prices

Throughout this book, prices for a two-course meal for one including a non-alcoholic beverage:

$$$$ = over Rp 300,000
$$$ = Rp 200,000–300,000
$$ = Rp 100,000–200,000
$ = below Rp 100,000

Batik scarves

SHOPPING

From modern malls and hinterland villages where traditional craftsmen sell their wares to the art galleries of Ubud and the silver emporia of Celuk, Bali has something to suit all shoppers' tastes.

The Balinese are renowned for their artistic skills, and you will find plenty of souvenirs to take home. As the range of local crafts, art, antiques, jewellery and clothes is so huge, it takes a bit of hunting and rummaging to find what's right for you.

Bartering

In markets, small shops and at street stalls, you are expected to haggle for your purchases where no price is indicated. Don't ask for an overly low price, as this will insult the vendor; ask instead how much the item costs, then whether this is the best price they can offer. Wait for the retailer to respond and never mention the amount of money you are prepared to pay. Tell them that this is more than you wanted to spend and ask if they could let you have the item for less. Continue this process for as long as the vendor offers a lower price. When they won't go any lower, thank them and head for the door. If they let you leave, that really was the best offer. Wait 15 minutes, go back, say you have reconsidered and will accept the last price.

KUTA

Jl Legian and Kuta Square present a hotchpotch of trendy branded outlets, souvenir shops, fashion boutiques and surfwear stores.

Discovery Mall, Bali Mal Galeria and Beachwalk

For a shopping mall excursion, you might want to visit the beachfront 'Discovery Mall', 'Bali Mal Galeria', or 'Beachwalk'. All three attract plenty of custom with global lifestyle branded boutiques, local retailers, souvenir and handicraft stores, food courts, cafés and restaurants. Discovery Mall and Bali Mal Galeria incorpo-

Lace shop in Seminyak

Kites for sale in Ubud market

rate department stores, while Beachwalk provides a dedicated kids' area and a digital format cinema with three studios.

KEROBOKAN AND SEMINYAK

In Kerobokan, you can rummage for treasures through cluttered little stores crammed with curios and antiques, browse classy homeware shops or wander through huge warehouses displaying their ranges of high-quality furniture.

In trendy Seminyak you will find a host of designer boutiques. Collections feature chic ethnic designs executed in richly garnished silks, diaphanous chiffons and strong, deep colours, perfect for Bali's glamorous night scene.

UBUD

If you are looking to purchase paintings, Ubud is the place to conduct your search. Classic, contemporary and abstract artworks, fine art, folk art and decorative wall panels can be found in the town's numerous galleries and art shops.

DENPASAR

Unadventurous consumers will not be attracted by the prospect of a shopping trip to Denpasar. However, if you are a bold and brave bargain-hunter, a spree within the heart of Bali's bustling provincial capital might prove to be the most rewarding experience of all. Visit Denpasar's vibrant markets, where every-thing and anything, including handicrafts and artwork, is available somewhere amid the chaos of the heaped stalls lining the crowded alleyways.

BALI'S HINTERLAND

Intrepid shoppers may also wish to visit the stone and woodcarving villages in Bali's hinterland. Batubulan is renowned for its stone carvings, which are exhibited along the main road, while the village of Mas is famous for woodcarving, its thoroughfare solidly lined with craft shops where you can watch the carvers at work.

TEGALLALANG

Alternatively, you could walk the 5km (3-mile) main street of Tegallalang, where you will find candles, mirrors, painted balsa-wood cats, flowers and frogs, batik lampshades, wrought-iron picture frames, banana-leaf boxes, dreamcatchers and bamboo wind-chimes galore, at half the price you would pay in Kuta.

CELUK

Visit the silver emporiums of Celuk, strung along 3km (2 miles) of main road flanked by a maze of backstreets chock-a-block with workshops and smaller outlets. Here, ornate silver jewellery, set with precious and semi-precious stones, are produced by master craftsmen whose sterling skills and trade secrets have been passed down through generations.

Legong dance performance at Ubud's Municipal Hall

ENTERTAINMENT

Bali is well known for its cultural entertainment. Theatre, dance, music and drama play a very important role in Balinese life, which in turn spills over into the island's many festivals.

Hindu ceremonies in Bali inevitably involve music and dance, which are performed as offerings designed to please the gods who are attending the ceremony, while also being enthusiastically enjoyed by the villagers. With the advent of tourism, the performing arts took on a new role in Bali. Dance troupes and music ensembles now have much more opportunity to be active, and are able to earn a living by performing at hotels and restaurants. Few places in the world can claim such a rich and varied environment of performing arts. This creative energy is also being harnessed in a bid to bring foreign creative talent to the island through festivals.

Dance

Balinese cultural performances are visual, entertaining and exciting, and can be appreciated by adults and children. There are numerous dance troupes on the island, and many different Balinese dance dramas exist, most of which have evolved from sacred rituals. The dances are often typified by subtle, controlled gestures and a fixed mask-like face with unfocused eyes and closed lips. The dancer's limbs form precise angles and the head sinks down so far that the neck disappears. At other times, gestures replicate nature, hands flutter like a bird in flight, and limbs follow sudden changes of direction as the performers move in slow, horizontal zigzagging circles. The eyes become expressive and beguiling as they flicker and dance, movements become jerky, sometimes provocative and occasionally erotic. Performances take place daily at tourist centres and are an integral part of almost every temple festival, accompanied by the shimmering, jangling, clashing, syncopated sounds of traditional Balinese gamelan music. Gamelan orchestras include gongs, metallophones (metal versions of xylophones), drums, cymbals and flutes. Many of the island's large hotels host cultural evenings two or three times a week.

FESTIVALS

Bali Arts Festival

The Bali Arts Festival is an annual fiesta of Balinese and Indonesian artistic traditions and culture. It lasts a full month and is held at Bali Arts Cen-

Gamelan orchestra

tre, Taman Budaya, in Denpasar. The festival showcases daily cultural performances, dance dramas, theatre, traditional and modern music, historical exhibitions, classical palace dances, handicraft exhibitions, garment and jewellery exhibitions, puppet shows, competitions and other related cultural commercial activities, presented by every region in Bali and beyond. The festival opens in June.

Bali Kite Festival

The Bali Kite Festival is held every year in July, when the winds are strong. It takes place at Padanggalak, Sanur, and is actually a seasonal religious festival intended to send a message to the gods for abundant crops and harvests. Traditional giant kites, measuring up to 4 by 10m (13 by 33ft) in size, are made and flown competitively by teams from different villages.

Ubud Writers and Readers Festival

The annual Ubud Writers and Readers Festival generally takes place in October. Lasting a few days, it comprises an action-packed programme of workshops, readings, keynote presentations, panel discussions, interviews, book launches, dance performances, poetry slams and lively literary lunches. The well-attended, highly regarded festival attracts literary artists, writers, readers, participants and observers from around the world.

Nusa Dua Festival

Nusa Dua sits on the eastern side of the Bukit. Usually held in October, the Nusa Dua Festival is a gala week of special events designed to engage the imagination of both the casual visitor and long-time lovers of Bali. The festival is officially opened with a grand parade before presenting some of Bali's finest performing arts, which include traditional dance, music and drama performances from other provinces across the Indonesian archipelago. Handicraft exhibitions and displays are also showcased. This festival has been a regular event since 1997 and is based on a theme that changes every year.

Negara Bull Races

Said to have originated as a simple ploughing competition, this extraordinary contest, which takes place on Sunday mornings from July through to October, features Bali's sleekest, most handsome water buffaloes. Each race involves two pairs of bulls running against each other around a 2km (1.25-mile) track. Each pair is hitched to a gaily painted wooden chariot driven by a precariously balanced, whip-happy jockey. Festooned with strings of bells, silks and decorative harness, every winning team gains a point for its club, with the most stylish contenders picking up bonus points for the splendour of their presentation.

Banana boat ride in Mushroom Bay

ACTIVITIES

Outdoor activities for all ages, from water sports and golf to horse riding and bird–watching, are plentiful in Bali. Specialist adventure tour companies take the adrenalin up a notch with a range of exciting excursions.

Bali presents a wealth of outdoor activities, not to mention adventure sports such as river rafting, mountain biking, jungle trekking and four-wheel-drive expeditions. Most companies provide a door-to-door pick-up and drop-off service, and just about every attraction on the island is child-friendly.

WATER SPORTS

Diving and snorkelling
Bali is the ideal location for learning to dive or diving for pleasure among some of the world's finest tropical reefs. The water is warm, and the marine life is abundant. Reputable dive schools, dive resorts and operators offer facilities, equipment and tuition for every PADI course, from beginners' discovery dives to the highest recreational level (see page 77).

Surfing
Bali is renowned as one of the great surfing meccas of the world, offering more than 20 top-quality breaks. The peak surf season is April through October, when the southeast trade winds blow offshore and the full force of the solid southern ocean swells hit the reefs around Kuta, Nusa Dua and the Bukit Peninsula. These are a great draw for veteran surfers, and the breaks found at Padang Padang and Uluwatu (see page 34), with its famous entry cave, are world-class barrelling reefbreaks. Meanwhile, for novices and surfers of intermediate ability, there are plenty of mellow beachbreaks.

Other water sports
Other water sports, such as wind-surfing and water-skiing, are easy to arrange in Bali. Hotels and tourist agencies/ information offices should have details.

OTHER ACTIVITIES

Fishing, eco-tours, bungy-jumping and four-wheel-drive or bike tours are among the activities on offer in Bali. The following may also appeal:

Bird-watching
The inland forests around Bedugul (see page 61) and Gunung (Mt) Batukau (see page 73) are abundant with birdlife. Of particular note are jewel-coloured kingfishers, a common sight along the island's many river banks.

Paraglider prepares for take off, Candidasa

Golf

Bali's five spectacular golf courses are all open to non-members and set in mountain, cliff-top and beach-side locations. The Handara Kosaido Country Club in Bedugul (see page 63) is located in the caldera of an ancient volcano and considered to be one of the most beautiful courses in the world.

Horse riding

There are several stables and equestrian resorts on the island offering riding adventures through rice fields, villages, monsoon forest, and along the beach. Most stables provide a good selection of well-trained horses of different sizes and varying temperaments to suit all ages and levels of experience.

Mountain cycling

Specialist adventure tour companies offer exciting mountain cycling tours, which also give an insight into the traditional Balinese lifestyle. Starting at around 1,100m (3,575ft) above sea level, each tour is an exhilarating descent through farms, hamlets and lush valleys, past ancient temples and beautiful rice fields. Each has a number of stops built in, allowing participants to sample some of the indigenous tropical fruits and spices and absorb the beauty of the region.

Paragliding

A number of paragliding clubs operate from the Bukit Peninsula, taking off from the cliff top some 80m (262ft) above Timbis beach, on the southernmost tip of the island. Harnessed to these non-motorised inflatable wings, it is possible to soar over everything from coral reefs to Hindu temples, and the views of the ridgeline are spectacular. Experience is not necessary, as tandem flights for all ages can be arranged with professional instructors and the latest equipment. The on-shore trade winds blow consistently from the southeast from June through September, making this ridge flyable on most days.

Trekking

The diversity of the island allows visitors anything from gentle hikes through rice fields, jungle, rainforests and national parks to challenging mountain treks in the dry season (see page 42). The trek between Lake Buyan and Lake Tamblingan is ideal for bird-watchers.

White-water rafting

White-water rafting is an action-packed journey through class II and III rapids, against an awesome backdrop of rainforest, gorges, rice terraces and dramatic waterfalls on the Ayung, Telaga Waja and Unda rivers. There are quite a number of different operators, the most reputable of which maintain exemplary safety standards with highly trained and experienced guides piloting the safety-equipped rafts. Hot showers at the end are followed by a buffet feast.

Artwork by I Nyoman Madia in Ubud's Museum Puri Lukisan

HISTORY: KEY DATES

Bali's strategic geographical location made it an important stopping point on the maritime trade route, which in turn brought about Dutch colonisation. Today, though, tourism is the island's biggest industry.

EARLY PERIOD AND MIDDLE AGES

2500–1500BC	Migrants from southern China and mainland Southeast Asia reach the archipelago and mix with aboriginal peoples.
300BC	Bronze-age culture in Bali.
AD78	Indian civilisation begins to make an impact.
500	Chinese traders mention the Buddhist kingdom of P'oli (Bali).
800	Buddhist Warmadewa dynasty rules Bali.
1000	Airlangga becomes king in East Java and his brother, Anak Wungsu, rules Bali (1035); Javanese influence increases in Bali. During civil war in Java, Bali becomes independent (1045).
1200	Javanese Singasari kingdom retakes Bali (1284); Kublai Khan attacks Java, and Bali breaks free again (1292).
1300	Javanese Majapahit kingdom conquers Bali (1343); Gelgel kingdom unifies Bali (1383).

MAJAPAHIT GOLDEN AGE

1400	Islam spreads to the archipelago and Majapahit begins to disintegrate; Bali becomes a haven for Hindu-Buddhists from Java.
1500	Golden Age for Bali under King Waturenggong; first Dutch arrive.
1600	Dutch East India Company sets up a trading post in Batavia (Jakarta), West Java. Civil war breaks out in Bali (1651); rebellion ends, and Klungkung (Semarapura) is founded (1681).
1700	Bali fractures into rival kingdoms, leading to continuous warfare; Bali controls East Java and Lombok.

EUROPEAN INFLUENCE

1839	Danish trader Mads Lange opens a trading port at Kuta.

President Sukarno and Major General Suharto in 1966

1849	North Bali is conquered through Dutch military force.
1894–6	Karangasem dynasty in Lombok and East Bali falls to the Dutch.
1898	The Dutch take control of Gianyar.
1900	The Dutch defeat royal families of Badung and Tabanan (1906), and Klungkung (1908).
1917	Devastating earthquake hits Bali.
1920–39	New artistic developments during the 1920s and 1930s.

WORLD WAR II AND INDONESIAN INDEPENDENCE

1942–5	Japanese Occupation during World War II; declaration of Republic of Indonesia on 17 August 1945, after Japanese surrender.
1945–9	Dutch create State of Eastern Indonesia that includes Bali; after war of independence, the UN recognises Indonesia, and Bali becomes a province.

POST-INDONESIAN INDEPENDENCE

1963	Gunung (Mt) Agung erupts, causing thousands of deaths and destroying many temples and villages.
1966	Suharto replaces Sukarno as president of Indonesia.
1986	Nusa Dua is developed into a high-class tourist resort area.
1998	Asian economic crisis hits Indonesia; riots in Jakarta leave over 500 dead. President Suharto resigns amid violent demonstrations.
1999	Rioting when Megawati Sukarnoputri, favoured candidate for president, is not selected; the situation calms when she becomes vice-president. Visitors and residents of other islands seek refuge on Bali when regional conflicts erupt.
2001	Megawati replaces President Abdurrahman Wahid, who resigns over corruption charges.
2002	Terrorist bombs in Kuta kill more than 200 people, mostly foreign tourists. Visitors stay away; many Balinese lose jobs.
2004	President Megawati loses re-election bid to Susilo Bambang Yudhoyono, after heavily contested polls run twice.
2005	On 1 October, three terrorist suicide bombs explode, one in Kuta Square and two on Jimbaran Beach. Twenty people are killed.
2012	A record year, with 2.88 million foreign visitors to Bali.

BEST ROUTES

1. Sanur, Denpasar and Uluwatu   28
2. Ubud Highlights   35
3. Batur and Kintamani   42
4. Bedulu, Tampaksiring
     and Tegallalang   45
5. Pejeng and Bangli   50
6. Klungkung and Besakih   53
7. Tenganan, Candidasa
     and Amlapura   56
8. Bratan and Bedugul   61
9. Lovina and Singaraja   66
10. Krambitan, Pupuan
     and Medewi   70
11. Tanah Lot, Jatiluwih
     and Batukau   73
12. Nusa Lembongan, Nusa
     Ceningan and Nusa Penida   77

The beach at Sanur

SANUR, DENPASAR AND ULUWATU

Drop by an expatriate artist's beach-front home, visit the museums and markets of Bali's capital city, mingle with monkeys, watch the sunset from a cliff-top perch and finish with a seaside seafood feast.

DISTANCE: 80km (50 miles)
TIME: A full day
START: Sanur
END: Jimbaran Bay
POINTS TO NOTE: This busy route is a good one for those staying in the south (ie Kuta, Seminyak, Sanur, Jimbaran or Nusa Dua). Hire a car and driver for the day; the driver will wait for you whenever you want to stop. Note that the centre of Denpasar involves some walking. Note, too, that the city markets and streets can be rather daunting if you are new to Bali; the Denpasar city element can be excluded from the route if preferred. Visitors interested in horticulture should follow this route on a Tuesday or a Friday, when the Bali Hyatt in Sanur conducts tours of its gardens.

This tour takes you from the historic village of Sanur to the markets and sights of the island's bustling capital, before heading down to a dramatic cliff-top temple and the surfing scene at Uluwatu, on Bali's southwest tip.

SANUR

The prosperous village of **Sanur** ❶ is synonymous with gracious living, vine-draped coral walls, majestic trees and a 5km (3-mile) golden sandy shoreline within a reef-sheltered lagoon, offering safe swimming, wakeboarding and windsurfing. A paved esplanade that runs the length of the beach was saved from erosion by an impressive landscaping and conservation project that has also safeguarded the coral reef.

Sanur was Bali's original tourist enclave, with the island's first simple guest rooms in the 1940s heralding the age of modern tourism. Today, the beach front is laced with a string of medium-range and luxury hotels, and the access roads are lined with numerous art and craft shops.

Bali Hyatt Gardens

Start with breakfast beside the beach at the **Bali Hyatt** ❷ (Jl Danau Tamblingan 89, Sanur; www.bali.resort.hyatt.com), after which you can stroll

Museum Le Mayeur

around the hotel's famous gardens, created by Australian landscape designer Made Wijaya – maybe participating in a guided tour (Tue and Fri 10am; free). An impressive series of terraces descends to a water garden and several other exquisite botanical and themed gardens, including a tropical white one inspired by the famous Sissinghurst Castle garden in Kent, southern England.

Museum Le Mayeur

Next stop is the **Museum Le Mayeur** ❸ (Jalan Hang Tuah, Pantai Sanur; Tue–Sun 8am–2pm; charge), located on Sanur beach north of the Grand Bali Beach Hotel.

The Belgian (Brussels) painter Adrien-Jean Le Mayeur de Merpres (1880–1958) lived in Bali from 1932 until shortly before his death in 1958. Sometimes described as Indonesia's answer

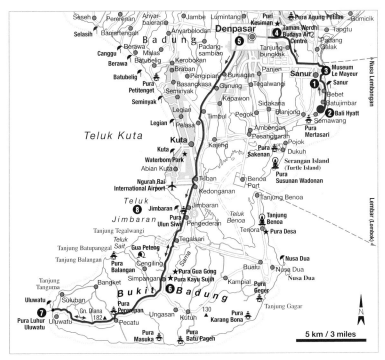

Volleyball on Sanur's beach

to Gauguin, Le Mayeur married the *legong* dancer, Ni Polok, a beauty who was only 16 when they met; he was 53. His only model, she appears numerous times, always bare-breasted, in his colourful Impressionistic paintings. Before his death, Le Mayeur donated to the government his studio-house with its few remaining works; it was then turned into a museum managed by Ni Polok until her death in 1986. The brackish sea air has unfortunately taken its corrosive toll on the paintings, but the house retains a lingering air of nostalgia.

Arts around town

From Sanur, take the main Denpasar road west for 6km (3.75 miles) and drop by the **Taman Werdhi Budaya Art Centre** ❹ (Jl Nusa Indah; Tue–Sun 8am–5pm; charge), home to an impressive collection of traditional and modern Balinese art, including Barong and Rangda dance costumes. From mid-June to July, the annual Bali Arts Festival takes place here, with daily performances, along with displays of arts and crafts from Bali and the Indonesian archipelago.

DENPASAR

Now head 2km (1.25 miles) further west into the city of **Denpasar** ❺, Bali's provincial capital. Originally known as Badung, the city is a growing metropolis characterised by winding alleyways, traffic jams, confusing signs, and illogical-seeming one-way streets. Many immigrants have settled here, including Chinese, Arab and Indian merchants. However, the old provincial kingdoms and villages of this densely populated area still function in the traditional way in terms of religious practice and local community government.

Museum Bali

Off Jalan Surapati, take a left turn to the **Museum Bali** ❻ (Jl Let. Kol Wisnu; Sat–Thur 8am–4pm, Fri 8.30am–1pm; charge), established in 1932 by German artist Walter Spies (1895–1942) for the preservation of traditional Balinese arts and crafts. The displays, in several pavilions from different parts of the island, include archaeological finds, dance masks, textiles, paintings and architectural illustrations of the Balinese temples, providing an unrivalled exhibition.

Pura Jagatnatha

Next door to the museum is **Pura Jagatnatha** ❼, a territorial temple built in 1953 and dedicated to Sanghyang Widhi Wasa, lord of the universe. Although the temple is open during daylight hours, you will probably not be allowed in (there isn't much to see); just peer through the gate at the white stone *padmasana* (lotus throne) topped by the gilded image of Sanghyang Widhi Wasa. The temple, which is popular among local people, embodies the importance given to monothe-

Wares on JL Sulawesi

Denpasar street scene

ism, as promoted by the Indonesian government.

Puputan Square

Across the street is **Puputan Square** 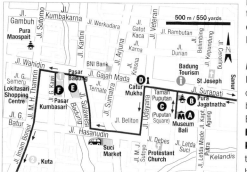 **C**, commemorating a suicidal battle of the Rajas of Badung against the Dutch Militia in 1906 and with a bronze memorial to those who lost their lives. At the square's northwest corner is the main intersection that leads to Veteran Street and all the major streets of Gajah Mada, with their rows of Chinese shops. In the middle of the intersection is the great **Catur Muka D** statue, representing Batara Guru, lord of the four directions. Four Hindu gods face in different directions: Mahadeva (west), Vishnu (north), Ishvara (east) and Brahma (south).

Streets of textiles and gold

You are now in the heart of Denpasar; not many visitors come this far into the city, but those who are prepared to brave the crowded streets and busy traffic will discover some unique shopping experiences. Not many people here speak English, but don't let that put you off: take time to enjoy the sights, sounds and aromas of this vibrant, historical city.

Walk 1km (0.5 miles) south down Jl Udayana and turn right into **Jl Hasanudin**, where Bali's gold (18–24 carat) shops are clustered. These shops are all very similar, but the Balinese designs are attractive, and the prices are much lower than in the West.

From here, cross the road north into **Jl Sulawesi**, Denpasar's fabric street, devoted to textiles of all descriptions. Shake off the commission hunters who will try to latch on to you, offering to be your guide, and make your own way to Jl Gajah Mada at the northern end of Jl Sulawesi. Turn left and pause at **Hongkong**, see **1**, for lunch; this extremely popular Chinese restaurant is frequented by expatriates as well as locals.

Marketplaces

Immediately to the west of Jl Sulawesi are the two biggest marketplaces in Bali, the chaotic **Pasar Badung E** and **Pasar Kumbasari F**, positioned along opposite banks of the polluted

Pasar Badung, Denpasar

Tukad Badung River. Pasar Badung is where the local people do their shopping, with the market's three floors dedicated to different products – ranging from fresh produce and flower petal offerings on the ground floor to dried foodstuffs and cooking utensils on the middle floor. The top floor specialises in items such as temple parasols, brass bells, baskets and garden tools. Pasar Kumbasari is another rabbit warren, with small shops specialising mainly in handicrafts, souvenirs and artworks.

If you're brave enough to eat where the locals eat, an alternative option for lunch as you drive out of Denpasar is **Sunda Kelapa**, see ①, situated on Jl Teuku Umar. Simple and cheap, this is a place to experience typical Jakartan cuisine. Be warned that the local beer may not be served cold.

THE BUKIT

Head back to the main road and travel south 55km (34 miles), skirting the resort areas of **Kuta** and **Seminyak** (see box right), past Jimbaran where we return for dinner (see page 34), all the way to the **Bukit Peninsula** ❻ and Pura Luhur Uluwatu.

Bali's lemon-shaped, southernmost peninsula is an arid limestone tableland that stands in sharp contrast to the island's lush, alluvial plains. Its dramatic coastline is pounded by a challenging surf that has made it a surfing mecca.

In the 1970s, Nusa Dua, on the southeast coast of the Bukit, was chosen as the location for the most ambitious resort project in Indonesia's history, resulting in a tourist enclave of wide paved lanes and manicured gardens, white-sand beaches, restaurants, a shopping mall, a conference centre and a golf course to support the five-star resorts.

It wasn't until much later, however, that the infrastructure of the rest of the peninsula improved sufficiently to support the development of its remote and magnificent cliff-edge sites. Since 2000, the Bukit has become the most upmarket destination on the island, with some of Bali's most opulent villas, glamorous private estates and boutique hotels.

Pura Luhur Uluwatu

Balanced on the edge of a narrow rocky cape on the southwestern edge of the peninsula is the 11th-century **Pura Luhur Uluwatu** ❼, the 'Lofty Headstone Temple'. Legend has it that the temple is actually a ship turned to stone. It was rebuilt by the Hindu priest Danghyang Nirartha, who came to Bali from Java in the 16th century following the spread of Islam there. It was from this cliff top that he is believed to have ascended into heaven after completing this last architectural wonder.

The site is particularly sacred to fishermen, who come here to pray to the sea goddess, Dewi Laut. A small

Padang Padang beach, Bukit

Pura Luhur Uluwatu is balanced on this cliff top

shrine with a statue of the priest and flanked by images of Brahma and Vishnu, Hindu gods of creation and life, are in the walled section to the left just as you enter.

The temple has two unusual gates, one a *candi bentar* (split gate) featuring relief carvings of birds topped by curved wings, and the other an arched structure with a monster face. Both gates are guarded on each side by two statues of Ganesha, the elephant-headed overcomer of obstacles and symbol of success.

A part of this long, narrow temple fell into the sea during the early 1900s, a premonition, it is said, of the impending Dutch massacre of Badung's royal family who had always maintained it. Numerous repairs have been made over the years, particularly in the late 1990s after the shrines were struck by lightning.

The views here at sunset are spellbinding, with fishing boats dotting the Indian Ocean. If you're lucky you might see turtles, dugong, manta rays and even whales swimming in the waters below.

Monkey business

The area around the temple is inhabited by a band of mischievous monkeys, who snatch unguarded items, so don't wear a hat, sunglasses, dangling earrings or anything else that can be yanked away. A traditional **kecak dance performance** takes place daily at 6pm (charge). Performed by around 100 male dancers, who are bare chested and hypnotically chant '*cak cak cak*', the dance depicts a battle in which Prince Rama is helped to defeat the evil King Ravana by the monkey-like Vanara – hence it is sometimes called the monkey dance.

Kuta and Seminyak

While Kuta and Seminyak are not stopovers on this route, both sit within the Bandung regency, north of the airport and southwest of Denpasar, and therefore cannot go without a mention. If you're looking for shopping, fine dining and a pulsating nightlife, consider making Seminyak your beach-side base, with Kuta a cheaper, less sophisticated option. Once a quiet fishing village, Kuta became the victim of years of unplanned development after being discovered by surfers in the 1960s. Nowadays, this hotchpotch of family-run guesthouses, bars, cafés, nightclubs, handicraft shops, surf emporia, money changers, beauty parlours and second-hand bookstores has a beach-party atmosphere. The 2002 Bali bombing is commemorated with a carved stone monument in Kuta, close to the site of the attack.

Trendy Seminyak, on the other hand, lays claim to the highest concentration of gourmet restaurants on the island, as well as numerous cocktail bars, nightspots, spas, designer boutiques, luxury villas and five-star hotels, that draw a glamorous crowd of visitors.

Kecak dance performed at Puru Luhur Uluwatu

Uluwatu Beach

An alternative idea for sunset is to drive out of the temple car park and turn left. Follow the road to the end, and walk down the steps to the line of cliff-edge *warungs* (food stalls/cafés). En route, check out **Uluwatu Beach** by descending more steep steps to the left. The sandy beach is accessible at low tide through a cave. Afterwards relax in one of the many surfer hang-outs on the cliff above and watch a spectacular sunset over an ice cold beer. Only the most proficient surfers dare to ride these waves.

JIMBARAN BAY

Another sunset option at the end of the route is to return along the main road leading back to the tourist centres and stop at the beautiful crescent-shaped **Jimbaran Bay** ❽ for a seafood feast of fish, shellfish and rice. There are dozens of seafood cafés serving the day's catch on the beach between the Four Seasons Resort and the airport. It's difficult to distinguish between them, but a consistently good one is **Menega Café**, see ❸. For a more upmarket dining experience, check out **Sundara**, see page 99, at the Four Seasons Resort.

Alternatively, if you're staying anywhere near Seminyak or Kerobokan and you'd rather eat closer to home, visit the street colloquially known as 'Eat Street', where you will be spoilt for choice. One of the most popular restaurants there is **Sarong**, see page 99.

Food and Drink

❶ HONGKONG

Jl Gajah Mada 99, Denpasar; tel: 0361-434845; daily 10am–10pm; $$
This respected Chinese restaurant has a faded grandeur, with fluted pillars and gaudy decor. Service is fast and the menu extensive, offering delicacies such as scallops, sea cucumber with Chinese mushrooms, crispy pigeon, frogs' legs, and banana *à la Sichuan*.

❷ SUNDA KELAPA

Jl Teuku Umar 183, Denpasar, tel: 0361-233481; daily 10am–11pm; $
In common with most *warungs* (stalls) in Denpasar, Sunda Kelapa is where the locals eat. The building and decor is basic, but the food at this long-established eatery is authentic Jakartan cuisine with over 50 different dishes.

❸ MENEGA CAFÉ

Jl Four Seasons, Muaya Beach, Jimbaran; tel: 0361-705888/mobile: 0812-39-33539; daily 11am–11pm; $$
Menega is one of Jimbaran's many seafood cafés, where fresh fish is displayed on ice for you to select. Minstrels serenade you as you enjoy your meal.

Barong mask at Puri Saren

UBUD HIGHLIGHTS

With so much to see around Ubud, this full-day driving and walking route has been designed to touch on a variety of sights and activities ranging from Balinese culture, art and history to scenic beauty and wildlife.

DISTANCE: 14km (9 miles) driving and 2km (1.25 miles) for the ridge walk
TIME: A full day
START: Ubud Market
END: Petulu or Puri Saren in Ubud
POINTS TO NOTE: This route offers a mix of walking and driving. You can either organise a car and driver for the day or use the transport men on the street as and when you need them. Negotiate a price before you set out and make sure the driver waits for you if you opt to visit Petulu at the end of the route. Wear comfortable walking shoes.

Ubud is Bali's cultural hub, a royal village situated at the confluence of two rivers on the southern edge of the island's cool mountainous foothills. A haven for local and foreign artists since the 1930s, it is the island's centre for fine arts and dance. In the surrounding villages you can watch the island's most accomplished painters, stonemasons, woodcarvers, mask makers and silversmiths at work. The name Ubud comes from the Balinese work *ubad* (medicine) because of the healing properties of plants growing by the Campuhan River on the western side of town.

CENTRAL UBUD

Ubud Market

Aim for an early start of 7–7.30am (breakfast is scheduled for later) to ensure that you experience the busy **Ubud Market ❶** (Jl Raya Ubud) before much of the fresh produce is whisked away to make room for tourist-oriented handicrafts. If you want to go shopping, plan to go back another day because you won't want to be carrying your purchases around with you on this route. As you walk through the narrow alleys, look out for the *daluman* stall, where the market's most respected lady mixologist prepares an ominous-looking dark green drink. If you sit at her trestle table, she will blend the mixture with a swirl of coconut milk, a drizzle of liquid palm

Statues at Puri Saren

sugar and a flourish that will convince you it's okay to drink. Look out, too, for the women serving vegetarian *bubur* – rice porridge slapped on a banana leaf and topped with roasted coconut, sprouts, greens and spicy *sambal* (chilli-based sauce).

Royal Palace

When you come out of the market, cross the street and peer in at the courtyard of **Puri Saren ❷** (corner of Jl Raya Ubud and Jl Suweta; free), the royal palace and home to the Sukawati royal family, one of several royal families in Bali. The public are welcome to stroll around during daylight hours, although there are no information signs. Built in the late 19th century, the palace is formed of a series of splendid pavilions with richly carved doors and incongruous colonial-era European and Chinese furniture. Most of the buildings were designed by I Gusti Nyoman Lempad

(c.1862–1978), Bali's most famous architect, artist and carver.

By now, you may be ready for a hearty breakfast. **Kafe Batan Waru**, see ❶, serves classy fare such as eggs Benedict on English muffins and wholegrain blueberry pancakes with maple syrup. To get there, go south down Jl Wanara Wana (Monkey Forest Road), opposite the palace, then take the first left into Jl Dewi Sita, where you will find the restaurant after about 250m/yds on the left-hand side. Alternatively, **Café Lotus**, see ❷, is 100m/yds west of the palace on Jl Raya Ubud, the main road. It has a romantic outlook over the beautiful lotus pond of **Pura Taman Sariswati ❸**, a temple built in the 1950s and dedicated to Dewi Saraswati, the goddess of learning, wisdom and the arts. Note the 3m (10ft) high statue here of Jero Gede Macaling, the demon lord of epidemics and pestilence. Amongst the

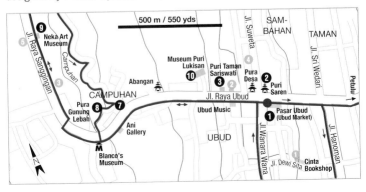

Barong masks and costumes

Ubud market

pink lotuses, water gushes out of the mouths of sculpted animals.

RIDGE WALK

The next part of this route is a delightful walk along the Campuhan Ridge, but to reach the starting point on the main road near **Kedewatan** ❹ (on the west side of Ubud), you will need a vehicle and driver, or a *bemo* (public minivan). Kedewatan village is famous for the fuzzy red fruit known as rambutan or buluan, similar to lychee. Buy some of these sweet fruits if they are in season, along with some bottled water.

From Kedewatan, follow the sign to **Pura Puncak Payogan** ❺, the 'Summit Temple of Meditation' at Payogan, where, during the 8th century, the holy man Resi Markandeya meditated after coming from Java, having followed a bright light to Bali. Just to the right, a narrow paved road winds down a river valley and up the other side to **Bangkiansidem** ❻ (Ant's Waist), named because this village lies on a narrow ridge between two broader sections.

The road ends at a paved footpath, so if you hire a car with a driver, ask him to wait at the staircase near the eastern end of the bridge in **Campuhan** ❼. Continue on the path for a leisurely 1km (0.5-mile) stroll with magnificent vistas of the countryside spreading out before you. The hillsides are covered with *alang alang* or *ambengan*, the grass that is used for thatching. Down below, you may be able to see people cutting out blocks of paras rock from the river banks. This compressed clay and volcanic ash is mostly used for carving statues and temple adornment.

Campuhan

On a clear day, you can see Gunung Agung, Bali's most revered volcano, rising majestically in the east – this was the source of the light that Resi Markandeya followed. At this point, take a look back at the view of palm trees and mountains.

Balinese temples

The temple or *pura* is the focus of the spiritual activity of every Balinese Hindu community on the island. They are specially designed without roofs to allow the gods easy access between the worlds, with the gates and walls serving to keep impure and evil influences away. Most villages on the island have at least three temples, and every home has a *merajan* (shrine) or *sanggah kemulan* (house temple). There are nine *kahyangan jagat* or directional temples in the province, and these are of major importance because they protect the entire island and its people. Other temples may be particularly significant because of their strategic clifftop or lakeside locations, their history, or their architectural beauty.

Ngaben (Funeral Ceremony) in Museum Puri Lukisan

The walk ends in Campuhan at **Pura Gunung Lebah** ❽, the 'Temple of the Low Mountain' referring to Gunung (Mt) Batur and dedicated to the lake goddess of Danau Batur. Resi Markandeya built his home at this holy site. Two rivers meet at Campuhan, meaning confluence, and the Balinese hold purification rituals here, such as the bathing of sacred temple relics and the dispersing of ashes of the cremated dead.

From the river, take the staircase up to the bridge. This is where your driver will be waiting, if you have hired one.

NEKA ART MUSEUM

Next en route is the **Neka Art Museum** ❾ (Jl Raya Sanginngan; www.museum neka.com; daily 9am–5pm; charge), which is just under 1.5km (0.75 mile) up the hill to the west. It was founded in 1976 by Suteja Neka, a schoolteacher-turned-art-collector. Here, a series of pavilions amid manicured gardens presents an outstanding collection of artwork showing the different historical styles of Balinese painting. Works by foreign artists, especially the Dutch-born Arie Smit, are a highlight, as are photographs from the 1930s. Look out for works by the late great Javanese artist, Abdul Aziz, whose subjects appear to lean out of their frames. Every piece has an informative label, so allow one or two hours to learn more about Balinese art and culture.

Afterwards, stop for lunch at **Indus**, see ❸, just 500m/yds down the hill from the art museum. The home cooking at this popular restaurant is superb, and the view from the open terrace of the mountain, the ridge and the river valley is magnificent.

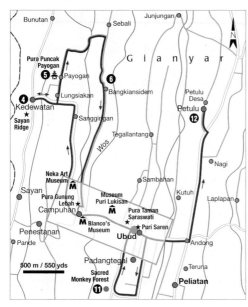

Neka Art Museum

The museum's garden pavilion

MUSEUM PURI LUKISAN

If you have time and would like to see more art, drop by the **Museum Puri Lukisan** ❿ (Jl Raya Ubud; www.museumpurilukisan.com; daily 9am–5pm; charge), set in attractive gardens with lotus ponds. To reach it, head east back towards the town for about 2km (1.25 miles), and you will find the museum set back from the road on the left-hand side. Founded in 1956, it features works by Balinese painters and carvers of the Pitamaha (Noble Aspiration), a famous artists' association in Ubud, which was active from 1936 to 1942. Fine drawings by I Gusti Nyoman Lempad, whose fluid classical scenes gained him the most recognition, works by the Young Artists from the 1960s, and temporary exhibitions complete the experience.

SACRED MONKEY FOREST

A fun activity, especially if you have kids, is a stroll through the **Sacred Monkey Forest** ⓫ (Padangtegal; daily 8am–6pm; charge). You'll need transport to get there, and it's a good idea to ask your driver to wait for you. From Puri Lukisan Museum, turn left and follow the road back to the royal palace and market. You can't turn into Monkey Forest Road in a four-wheeled vehicle because it is a one-way street, so instead take the first turning after the market into Jl Hanoman and follow the road all the way down to the bottom of the hill, where you will see the entrance. This holy area and important ecological reserve is home to a band of about 300 long-tailed, grey Balinese macaques. They can be very

History of art in Bali

Art is omnipresent in Bali, finding its roots in the symbolically decorative adornment of palaces and temples, making it inseparable from courtly life and spiritual practice. For centuries, artists, artisans and craftsmen worked under the patronage of the priests and the ruling classes, decorating the royal courts with carved wooden panels, paintings, silk wall hangings and stone sculptures. These artists of old never signed their work – paintings were produced collaboratively and anonymously, with the men usually living close together in artists' villages.

Things changed in the 1920s and 1930s, with the arrival of avant-garde foreign artists, such as Walter Spies, Rudolf Bonnet, Arie Smit (see page 38) and Adrien-Jean Le Mayeur (see page 29), who encouraged individual freedom of expression, while also introducing Western painting concepts. A second movement occurred in the early 1960s, when Arie Smit encouraged the artists of Penestanan to explore and experiment with vivid colours and simpler abstract forms.

Dance at Pura Gunung Lebah

mischievous, but they are interesting to observe, especially with their young. The Balinese regard the monkeys as the sacred descendants of the monkey general Hanoman.

Other attractions here include three temples, which are accessible via the paved pathways: the holy bathing temple (down a long flight of steps next to a river); Pura Prajapati, the funeral or cremation temple; and the important Pura Dalem Agung Padangtegal with its ornately carved gate. The latter is dedicated to Durga, goddess of death.

PETULU

You will now need a driver to take you to the tiny village of **Petulu** ⑫; aim to arrive around 5.30pm. To get there, head back up Monkey Forest Road, turn right and follow the main road to the end, where there is a big statue. Turn left and head up the hill. The road to Petulu is on the left-hand side after about 2km (1.25 miles), heralded by a painting of a white heron. Another 1km (0.5 miles) brings you into the village, which is famous because every evening at sunset thousands of white Javan pond herons and plumed egrets come to roost for the night. It's a spectacular sight, as the flocks of birds fill the sky before landing, squabbling over prime perches and turning the tree tops white.

Village tradition dictates that the birds should not be disturbed during their roosting, but you can sit at a simple viewing platform, and drink cold Bintang beers or soft drinks as you watch. Local legend tells that there were no herons in the village of Petulu until after the political backlash that followed the attempted Communist coup of 1965, when tens of thousands of men and women were murdered. Ask any of the elders in the village, and they will tell you that the birds appeared after one of the worst of the massacres, and are believed to be the souls of the slaughtered.

DANCES AND DINNER

An alternative to the Petulu herons is an early evening Balinese dance performance in the courtyard of **Puri Saren**, the Royal Palace (corner of Jl Raya Ubud and Jl Suweta; starts at 7pm; charge), by far the best and most dramatic setting for the performing arts in Ubud. One of the most famous dances is the *legong* dance, which is performed here every evening along with some other dances. The *legong* dance – a quintessential display of Balinese grace and femininity, performed by three young girls – is the most refined of all the temple dances. There are various forms of this dance, the most common being the *legong karaton*, based on a classic 12th-century tale from Java about a princess held captive by a wicked king.

Dinner options in the town are plen-

Sacred Monkey Forest   *Legong dance, Municipal Hall, Ubud*

tiful. **Terazo**, see ④, on Jl Suweta, near the palace, is a popular hang-out, while **Mozaic** (see page 101), located near Neka Art Museum, offers gourmet dining. Also on this stretch is the famous **Naughty Nuri's**, see ⑤, with an atmosphere evocative of an English pub, and a daily barbecue.

Food and Drink

① KAFE BATAN WARU

Jl Dewi Sita; tel: 0361-9775288; www.bali goodfood.com/Batanwaru; daily 8am– midnight; $$

Styled after a colonial teahouse with tea chairs and a collection of rare lithographs and prints, this restaurants serves authentic Indonesian dishes such as Grandma Atik's 'Ikan Acar Kuning' (fish steaks in a turmeric sauce with peppers and pickled garlic), international food and superb breakfasts.

② CAFÉ LOTUS

Jl Raya Ubud; tel: 0361-975660; www.lotus-restaurants.com/cafe-lotus-ubud; daily 8.30am–11pm; $$

This landmark restaurant has a gorgeous outlook over a lotus pond; a frame of gnarled frangipani trees with a temple backdrop completes the picture. Serves delicious pastas and desserts, as well as energy-booster drinks.

③ INDUS

Jl Raya Sanggingan; tel: 0361-977684; www.casalunabali.com/indus-restaurant; daily 9am–11pm; $$

An Ubud favourite, with stunning views of the Tjampuhan River valley and Gunung (Mt) Agung from its terraces and cool open-sided interior. Serves healthy Asian cuisine, including Indian chickpea curry, and Indonesian *nasi campur*, comprised of red rice and a selection of vegetables, meat or fish, and other accompaniments such as the fried soya bean cakes known as *tempe*. There is also a small art gallery on the premises.

④ TERAZO

Jl Suweta; tel: 0361-978941; www.baligood food.com/terazo; daily 10.30am–midnight; $$$

This semi open-air restaurant and bar is flanked by ponds with dining on two levels under a soaring roof. The contemporary Asian and Mediterranean-style cuisine is slightly upmarket, and the vibe is friendly and casual yet hip.

⑤ NAUGHTY NURI'S

Jl Raya Sanggingan; tel: 0361-977547; daily 9am–11pm; $$

A favourite with Ubud's expats, drawn by the potent Martinis, this street-side semi open-air *warung*-style pub is always busy. You can order steaks, lamb chops, ribs and sausages from the barbecue, or choose from a limited selection of Indonesian dishes from the menu.

BATUR AND KINTAMANI

In this route, a good day trip from Ubud, highlights include descending into a volcanic caldera, climbing the active volcano in the centre of the caldera or just relaxing in the hot springs at the crater lake.

DISTANCE: 19km (12 miles)
TIME: A full day if you climb the volcano or a more leisurely half day if you don't.
START: Kintamani
END: Pura Puncak Penulisan
POINTS TO NOTE: If you plan to climb the volcano, leave as early as possible to avoid the midday heat (you may prefer to do the sunrise trek, which begins around 4am). Wear good walking shoes and bring hats, sunscreen and bottled water. Don't attempt this during the rainy season (Nov–Mar), as it can get dangerously slippery. Batur and the Kintamani area are located about 30km (18 miles) from Ubud, so this tour could follow on from the Ubud Highlights trip (route 2) and the Pejeng and Bangli route (No. 5).

Tourists flock to Kintamani, typically to enjoy an Indonesian buffet lunch at one of the many panoramic restaurants that overhang the ancient volcanic crater rim. The caldera is 14km (8.75 miles) across at its widest diameter, and in the middle is the black cone of Gunung Batur, a volcano that puffs out steam and has erupted more than 20 times in the last 200 years. At its foot is the crescent-shaped Danau Batur, the island's largest lake. Its depth has never been recorded, but the lake is the source of most of the rivers in the eastern half of Bali.

PENELOKAN

Take the road north out of Ubud through Payangan and drive 32km (20 miles) up to the village of **Kintamani ❶**, set on the rim of a huge, ancient caldera. Turn right along the scenic road that follows the crater rim for 3km (1.75 miles) to **Penelokan ❷**, meaning 'viewpoint' because of the stunning view of the volcano and lake.

At Penelokan, visit **Batur Volcano Museum** (Jl Kintamani, Penelokan; www.baturmuseum.com; daily 9am–5pm; charge), where you can learn about volcanic phenomena through information panels, interactive games and computer simulations, as well as

Gunung Batur volcano

three 20-minute films. The museum is fun to visit with children.

TOYA BUNGKAH

Wind 8km (5 miles) down through lava fields to **Toya Bungkah ❸**. This lakeside fishing village, one of eight *bintang danu* (stars of the lake), has grown as an accommodation centre and is the main start point for treks up Gunung Batur.

GUNUNG BATUR

Gunung Batur is 1,717m (5,635ft) high, but the upper cone is only 700m (2,275ft) above the level of the lake and can be climbed and descended in a few hours. A local cartel actively discourages independent trekkers by not allowing people to hike alone, so you will need to hire a licensed guide. 'Official' fees for guides are high, but much cheaper deals can be negotiated at some of the guesthouses and restaurants at the lake.

The strange landscape is punctuated with hillocks and a series of craters with jets of white steam puffing out of small holes. On a clear day, you will be rewarded with a beautiful view of the lake, Mt Abang, Mt Agung, the distant sea and Mt Rinjani in Lombok. The surface is loose and sandy here, and at the top there's a warm crust of ground, so be careful where you tread. Ask your guide to prepare a meal of baked bananas and hard-boiled eggs cooked to perfection in the natural heat belching from the belly of the volcano (you may need to ask them in advance to do this).

DANAU BATUR

After the descent, the hot springs at Toya Bungkah, on the shore of **Danau Batur**, are perfect for easing aching limbs – though the rest of the lake is cold, the water here can be close to scalding. Frequented mostly by locals, the public bathing spot is free of charge but polluted, since many people use soap.

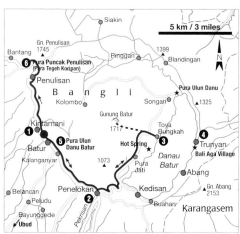

Prayers at Pura Ulun Danu Batur

Recommended is the **Tirta Sanjiwani** (daily 8am–5pm; charge), with two hot-spring pools and a regular swimming pool in a lovely garden above the lake.

Afterwards, have lunch at nearby **Nyoman Mawa 'Under the Volcano'** (see page 102), which has excellent crispy fried fish from the lake *(mujahir)*, served with chilli-onion relish. Alternatively, back up on the rim are restaurants catering to busloads of tourists; one of the best is at **Lakeview Hotel** (see page 102).

TRUNYAN

Look across the lake and on the eastern shore you will see the isolated village of **Trunyan ❹**. The residents are Bali Aga people, who inhabited the island long before the 14th-century Majapahit invasion and sought refuge from imperialistic strangers. Today, the people still retain a social order aligned with ancient traditions. Among their rules is that cremation should not be practised here. Instead, in a shadowy cemetery some 500m/yds outside the village and accessible only by boat, the bodies of the dead are wrapped in cloth and left in bamboo cages on the ground. Strangely, there is no smell, due to the presence of a Taru Menyan tree, believed to produce a fragrant odour, while its roots, beneath the bodies, bafflingly prevent putrefaction. Only the brave visit Trunyan. Most visitors are discouraged by tales of touts demanding extortionate boat fares that increase halfway across the lake. However, the village is now accessible by a narrow, winding and incredibly steep road; it is possible to go by car but probably safer by *ojek* (motorcyle taxi), which can be arranged in Toya Bungkah.

TEMPLE TOUR

Now return to Penelokan via the rim and drive 4km (2.5 miles) north to **Pura Ulun Danu Batur ❺** (donation), Bali's second most important temple complex. Unlike other temples, it is always open and has a permanent staff of 24 priests; selected as children by a virgin priestess, they serve for life. The temple was relocated here in 1926 when lava flows destroyed the original one at the edge of the lake. The largest temple, Pura Penataran Agung Batur, is dedicated to the lake goddess; the gates are towering architectural masterpieces.

Pura Puncak Penulisan

Drive a further 3km (1.75 miles) uphill past Kintamani to **Pura Puncak Penulisan ❻** (also known as Pura Tegeh Koripan; open daylight hours; donation), Bali's highest temple. Climb the long staircase to this ancient 'High Life Temple' shrouded by mists. Here, you'll see statues of ancient deified kings and queens, carved between the 10th and 14th centuries. On clear days, the views are spectacular.

Goa Gajah

BEDULU, TAMPAKSIRING AND TEGALLALANG

This busy day route covers an area southeast and east of Ubud. Sights include a holy cave, two temple complexes, funerary monuments, holy springs, terraced rice fields, woodcarving shops and the Elephant Safari Park.

DISTANCE: 40km (25 miles)
TIME: A full day
START: Bedulu
END: Taro
POINTS TO NOTE: There are a lot of sights to cover, so you may choose to focus only on some of them. The elephant park could be omitted at the end, but it is highly recommended, especially for families with children. Bring hats, sunscreen and bottled water.

This route begins 5km (3 miles) southeast of Ubud, in a region heavy with ancient archaeological sites and old temples. It then heads to the Tampaksiring area, where highlights include a cluster of ancient temples, before continuing to Tegallalang (Grass Fields), known for its rice terraces that spill down a river gorge. Northwest of Tegallalang is the village of Taro, home to the family-friendly Elephant Safari Park. Taro is also where Bali's sacred albino buffalo comes from.

AROUND BEDULU

After an early breakfast, head south out of Ubud through Peliatan. From here, follow the main road as it turns east for 2km (1.25 miles) to **Bedulu ❶** (or Bedahulu) and Goa Gajah. Bedulu village is positioned on the banks of the Petanu River. Despite its small size it is steeped in history and surrounded by some of Bali's most notable and ancient wonders. Ubud's best known artist, I Gusti Nyoman Lempad, was born here in 1862 and lived to be 116; he built and carved many of Bedulu's temple gates and shrines. The *kecak* dance (see page 33) was also devised in Bedulu in the 1930s.

Goa Gajah

Descend the steps into the **Goa Gajah ❷** (Elephant Cave; daily 9am–5pm; charge), which dates from the 11th century and is carved out of solid rock. Just above the cave entrance is a monstrous head (possibly mistakenly identified as an elephant's head), known as Bhoma and believed to frighten away evil.

Pura Samuan Tiga

The interior is in a T-shape. At the left (western) end is a four-armed stone image of Ganesha, the elephant-headed Hindu god of making things happen and remover of obstacles. To the right are three *lingga* (phallic images of Shiva, Hindu god of destruction and reincarnation) with eight smaller ones around each, all on a common base and carved from a single stone.

In front of the cave is a former bathing place with steps leading down to separate areas for men and women. Water pours out of jars held by four voluptuous female stone figures flanking two chunky males, whose upper halves once stood outside the cave entrance. In 1954 a Dutch archaeologist excavated the area and uncovered the matching lower halves of the statues. Behind this is Pura Taman, a modern temple with a shrine in a pond.

South of the bathing place are steps leading down to the Petanu River, which was once known as Lwa Gajah – 'Elephant River'.

Pura Samuan Tiga

Return to the main road and continue east for 1km (0.5 miles) beyond the intersection to **Pura Samuan Tiga** ❸ (daylight hours; donation). This vast 'temple of the meeting of the three parties' stages an 11-day ceremony during the 10th full moon; it is the third most important temple in Bali and was the state temple of the Warmadewa dynasty, which ruled until the 14th century. The name may refer to the blend of animism, Buddhism and Hinduism practised in Bali today.

There are dozens of shrines here, built on a series of terraces; some house

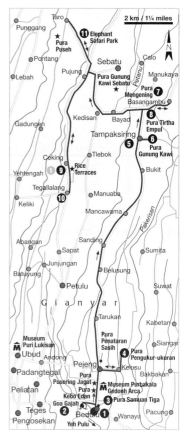

Festival preparations   *Carvings on coconut shells, Tampaksiring*

ancient stone figures of deities and phallic images. The temple has undergone continuous renovation since 1994 but still retains an atmosphere of awe and power. Festivals here involve huge processions, ritual dances and mock battles.

Under a soaring banyan tree are three multi-tiered brick-and-stone *meru* (pagodas), structures usually made of wood and thatching found in most Balinese temples. From north to south (left to right), these are dedicated to the deities of the lakes, wealth and sea, representing the upper, middle and lower realms of the spiritual world. People usually pray here for material success. Some pavilions house ancient sculptures of the goddess of death – Durga trampling the buffalo demon, phallic representations of the god of destruction, Shiva, and other Hindu deities.

Pura Pengukur-ukuran

Continue on the narrow road going east past the temple and follow it north for 4km (2.5 miles) through Petemon and Sawagunung all the way to the 12th-century temple complex of **Pura Pengukur-ukuran ❹** (daylight hours; donation). Rich carvings adorn the walls and gates of this so-called 'Temple of Measurements'. Walk down a steep flight of enormous stone steps to the river; this is a quiet place with an air of mystery and a good place to cool off. There are three small niches nearby, one with some statues. Examine the arrangement carefully, for villagers say

that if you look again later, the figures may have shifted places by themselves.

A small path downstream leads you up to the main road. Backtrack 2km (1.25 miles) south and turn right at a junction that takes you the same distance west. The road emerges at the main intersection in Pejeng.

TAMPAKSIRING

From here, turn right and continue north for 13km (8 miles) uphill to **Tampaksiring ❺**. This district is home to numerous woodcarvers and the Presidential Palace (one of three in Indonesia), which was built in the late 1950s for President Soekarno and is now used as an occasional presidential residence.

You'll see a sign on your right for **Pura Gunung Kawi ❻** (daily 9am–5pm; charge), a blinding green water canyon surrounded by swaying fields of tall, indigenous, Balinese rice, known as 'Padi Bali'. Approached via a long, steep run of steps, this is one of the prettiest places on the island. Gaze in wonder at 10 ancient royal shrines dedicated to 11th-century Balinese royalty, carved out of the rock face of the gorge of the Pakerisan River. This 'Mountain Temple of Poets' is a memorial to King Anak Wungsu of the Warmadewa dynasty. They are not tombs, however, as none of the ashes of the cremated bodies was deposited here. The 7m (23ft) -high carvings resemble 9th-century Javanese *candi* (memorial shrines).

Intricate carvings on cattle bones

A cluster of four *candi* on the west bank are monuments to the king's minor consorts, while five more across the river are for the king, queen and important family members. Water flows through small channels and pours out from spouts into a pool that once served as a royal bath.

Located nearby is a cluster of niches and enclosed rooms, also cut from solid rock; these may once have been a Buddhist monastery. Remove your footwear before entering.

Rice farming

The intensely productive *sawah* (rice fields) of Bali are a thousand years old, as are the democratic irrigation co-operatives, or *subak*, that manage them. Rural life is dependent on the accuracy of the water flow as it is diverted from the rivers and streams that gush from the crater lakes in Bali's central highlands. Through ancient, yet sophisticated, systems of aquatic engineering (including canals, tunnels and bamboo pipes), combined with elaborate social structures, the *subak* control the flow of water to ensure its even distribution to Bali's farmers. Using gravity, water is channelled into the uppermost *sawah* before flowing downhill to supply each farm in turn. The *subak* are not only responsible for the maintenance of the tunnels and aqueducts, but also the coordination of the rice planting.

Pura Mengening

Return to the main road and continue 1km (0.5 miles) north to a crossroads and turn right. A sign on your right indicates a road to **Pura Mengening** ❼ (daylight hours; donation), a small 'Clear Water Temple', with a holy spring under a banyan tree. Nearby is a larger, renovated temple with a restored ancient building inside resembling the temple facades at Pura Gunung Kawi.

Pura Tirtha Empul

Return to the main road and continue to nearby **Pura Tirtha Empul** ❽ (daily 8am–6pm; charge), a 10th-century holy spring and temple. Possessing magical powers and believed to be the elixir of immortality, the freshwater springs bubble up into a large tank within the temple and gush out through water spouts into a bathing pool, where elaborate carvings adorn the lichen-covered walls.

TEGALLALANG

Backtrack 500m/yds to a small crossroads and instead of bearing left (south) on the main road, go west for 3km (2 miles) until you meet the main Tegallalang–Ubud road. If a late lunch, spectacular views and handicraft shopping is on your agenda, turn left and head south, stopping after 4.5km (2.75 miles) at **Kampung Café**, see ❶, in **Ceking** ❾ to eat and take in the dramatic view of rice terraces.

Continue south for 1km (0.5 miles) to

Tegellalang rice terraces　　　　　　　　　*Holy springs at Pura Tirtha Empul*

take a closer look at this sculpted landscape in **Tegallalang** ⑩. This is a 5km (3-mile) -long street of woodcarving workshops and simple wholesale outlets, where you can buy wooden handicrafts and bamboo wind-chimes galore, at half the price you would pay in Kuta.

Elephant Safari Park

Alternatively, if you would prefer to spend the afternoon interacting with elephants, turn right at the point where you meet the main Tegallalang–Ubud road and head north for 500m/yds. Turn left at the junction and follow the signs to the **Elephant Safari Park** ⑪ (Jl Elephant Park Taro, Tegallalang; daily 8am–6pm; charge), which enjoys a cool jungle setting next to the remote village of **Taro**. This ancient village marks the centre of the island. According to legend, this was where the 8th-century itinerant Javanese priest Rsi Markandya was sent by the gods on a mission to establish a settlement. It is also where Bali's sacred albino buffalo come from.

The park provides sanctuary for 35 Sumatran elephants. The Sumatran elephant – the world's smallest and possibly oldest elephant species – once roamed freely in a diverse habitat untouched by man. Over the last few decades, however, the population of this little-known species has rapidly and tragically declined, due to increased illegal logging and the destruction of rainforests to make way for palm-oil plantations. This leaves the Sumatran

elephant as one of the rarest, most highly endangered elephant species.

Here, adults and children can enjoy the wonderful and unforgettable experience of meeting, hand-feeding, stroking and observing these amazing, highly intelligent creatures, rescued from the Indonesian island of Sumatra. You can even ride the elephants on a safari tour through the park and watch elephant talent shows (11.45am, 1.45pm, 3.45pm daily).

A great asset for Bali, the park is regarded as the best of its kind in the world and is an exceptional example of ecotourism. There is a restaurant here (see page 102), which makes a good alternative venue for lunch. You can also stay overnight here at the **Safari Park Lodge**, or return to Ubud for dinner, where a good choice might be **Lamak** (see page 101).

Food and Drink

① KAMPUNG CAFÉ

Ceking, Tegallalang; tel: 0361-901201; daily 8am–10pm; $$
This rustic restaurant clings to the edge of the Sapat river valley, with fine views of the rice terraces down the side of the gorge. Fresh ingredients are used to create superb Indonesian and Western dishes including *kare ayam*, chicken curry with vegetables, pineapple and rice, or *gado-gado*, steamed vegetables and potato with peanut sauce, boiled egg and rice.

'Moon of Pejeng' kettledrum

PEJENG AND BANGLI

Highlights on this route, which heads northeast of Ubud, include the world's largest kettledrum, erotic temple sculptures, an archaeological museum, dramatic relief carvings and the terraces of an imposing temple.

DISTANCE: 31km (19 miles)
TIME: A full day
START: Pejeng
END: Kota Gianyar
POINTS TO NOTE: This trip can follow on from route 3 as well as being done more or less in reverse starting at Bangli. Alternatively, it can be combined (on separate days) with route 4. There are some steps to climb, although nothing too strenuous. If you are staying in Ubud, you should be able to find a driver in the town. Note that there are no international-standard restaurants or cafés on this route, so you may wish to pack a picnic. Alternatively, stop at one of the small, basic local *warungs* (stalls) passed en route, although the choice at these will be limited.

This route winds through the ancient Pejeng-Bedulu kingdom, where there are numerous notable relics, and ends in the sleepy town of Bangli, the former capital of another ancient kingdom.

PEJENG

The journey begins in the village of **Pejeng** ❶, 4km (2.5 miles) east of Ubud, named after an illustrious kingdom that was concentrated in this area from the 9th to the 14th centuries. Here you will find **Pura Panataran Sasih** ❷, or 'Temple of the Moon', which contains the celebrated bronze gong, or kettledrum, known as the 'Moon of Pejeng'. Said to be more than 2,000 years old, it is the largest in the world.

Pura Pusering Jagat

From here it is a short walk south down the main road to **Pura Pusering Jagat** ❸, a large temple famous for its realistic stone *lingga* and *yoni* (images of the male and female sexual organs). Childless couples come here to pray for children. Nearby is a big cylindrical stone vessel carved with images of gods and demons churning the elixir of life in a scene from the 5,000-year-old Hindu epic, the *Mahabaharata*. A depression in the ground nearby is the navel of this 'Temple of the Navel

Inside Pura Panataran Sasih　　　　　　　　　　*Carvings at Yeh Pulu*

of the Universe'. Offerings placed here vanish, allegedly reappearing far away at Pura Dalem Ped on Nusa Penida, off the southeast coast (see page 80).

Temple of the Crazy Buffalo

Down the road is **Pura Kebo Edan** ❹ (daylight hours; donation). This 'Temple of the Crazy Buffalo' is famous for its large 14th-century statue of a masked giant with serpent-entwined legs dancing on a demon. His equally giant penis swings to the left, symbolic of the Tantric ritual indulgence of forbidden acts.

Museum Purbakala Gedong Arca

Keep going south a short distance to **Museum Purbakala Gedong Arca** ❺ (Tue–Sun 8.30am–2pm; charge), a small archaeological museum that showcases ancient pre-Hindu artefacts, stone carvings and old Chinese porcelain. The most fascinating exhibits are large stone sarcophagi with protruding heads on the upper and lower halves. These ancient coffins show that prehistoric Balinese buried their dead before Buddhists and Hindus introduced cremation.

YEH PULU

By car, continue south 3km (2 miles) into **Bedulu** (Bedahulu; see page 45), crossing the bend in the main road. At the end of the road, walk on a paved path through rice fields to **Yeh Pulu** ❻. Adorning a rock wall are large narrative relief carvings believed to have been created in the 14th century by the legendary Balinese giant, strongman and master builder, Kebo Iwa, using his fingernails.

Pura Kehen temple

KUTRI

Backtrack all the way to the bend in the main road and turn right, heading 2km (1.25 miles) east to **Semabaung**. Turn right again at the traffic lights to reach nearby **Kutri ❼**, home to a cluster of three temples: Pura Puseh, Pura Bukit Dharma, and Pura Kedharman. Climb the steps up a small hill to see a dramatic statue of Hindu goddess Durga slaying a buffalo demon.

BANGLI

The regency and town of Bangli is located in the foothills of the Batur volcanic range. Due to its proximity to Lake Batur, a major source of irrigation water for south and east Bali, the regency was fought over by neighbouring rulers. Bangli became the capital of this Balinese kingdom in the Balinese Icaka year of 1204.

From here go back to the traffic lights and bear right, staying on the main road and heading east for 3km (2 miles). At the next junction, turn left to reach **Kota Gianyar** (Gianyar City) **❽**, the capital of a former powerful kingdom and famous for its woven textiles. For now, drive through the town centre – we'll return here later. After you leave the town, take the first turning (a major junction) on the left, heading north for 8km (5 miles) to **Bangli**.

Just north of that town, take a winding road to the right (west) for 1km (0.5 miles) towards **Bukit Demulih ❾**. This

is the 'Hill of No Return', so-named for its beautiful views, which will make you reluctant to leave.

Pura Kehen

However, do go back to the main road and head east to **Pura Kehen ❿** (daily 9am–5pm; charge), the state temple of the Bangli kingdom and the second largest in Bali. It is also one of the island's most beautiful and impressive temples, built during the 11th century and set on a wooded hillside with terraces lined with religious statues. The imposing entrance, with its fabulously carved doors depicting grotesque demons, is flanked by elephant heads, while the temple itself has dozens of shrines and an 11-tiered *meru* (pagoda) dedicated to Shiva.

KOTA GIANYAR

Return to the main road and backtrack to **Kota Gianyar**. By late afternoon, the streets by the town market will be lined with stalls for the night fair. Browse and try some local food such as *babi guling*, Bali's famous slow cooked, spit-roasted pig with hot sauce, smoked chicken and Balinese sweets, or head back to Ubud (see route 2) for classier restaurant fare.

For a special treat, you may like to dine at one of the boutique hotels on the Ayung River Gorge, such as **Ubud Hanging Gardens** or **Four Seasons Sayan** (see pages 90 and 91), both of which have stunning views.

The Kerta Gosa, Klungkung

KLUNGKUNG AND BESAKIH

Visit the former Royal Courts of Justice in Klungkung, continue to the 'Mother Temple' on the slopes of Bali's highest and holiest mountain, then descend through stunning rice terraces to a weaving village.

DISTANCE: 43km (26 miles)
TIME: Half day or a leisurely day
START: Klungkung
END: Sidemen
POINTS TO NOTE: There's nothing too arduous about this route, apart from the steps at Pura Besakih and the rather aggressive hawkers – to avoid these, find a driver who will also act as your guide. This route takes you from the Klungkung Regency into the Karangasem Regency; it won't involve too much driving if you are based in Ubud or Candidasa, and it can be combined (on separate days) with routes 2 (Ubud) or 7 (Tenganan, Candidasa and Amlapura).

The villages of the Klungkung and Karangasem regencies, in the east, are among the most beautiful in Bali. This route takes you through some of these villages after visiting an historic royal capital, followed by Pura Besakih, the largest and most sacred site on the island.

KLUNGKUNG

This tour starts in **Klungkung** ❶ (also known as Semarapura), meaning 'happiness' or 'beauty'. The town is the royal capital of Bali's smallest regency and in 1908 was the last kingdom to hold out against the Dutch. The king of Klungkung led 200 hopelessly outnumbered members of his family and court into a *puputan* (ritual suicide), in the face of the Dutch guns. Most of **Puri Semarapura** (Fortress of Love Palace; daily 9am–5pm; charge) was destroyed at the time, but in Taman Gili, the gardens of the former palace, the 300-year-old **Kerta Gosa** (Royal Courts of Justice) and **Bale Kembang** (floating pavilion) still stand. Bale Kambang rests on a giant stone 'turtle' that appears to float in the middle of a pond.

Further back is the **Kori Agung** (main gate) of the palace. Look for Chinese, Portuguese and Dutch figures on it alongside demons and animals. The wooden doors were said to have shut by themselves after the *puputan*, and no one has been able or dared to open

Ceiling detail in Kerta Gosa

them since. The **museum** next to this displays temple artefacts, photographs, dance costumes and textiles from Klungkung. Across the street is the towering black **Puputan Klungkung Monument** that commemorates the *puputan*.

PURA BESAKIH

From the main crossroads at Klungkung, head north 21km (13 miles) to **Pura Besakih ❷** (daily 7am–6pm; charge, plus extra charge for cameras), known as the 'Mother Temple'. This is the larg-

est and most important temple complex on Bali, situated on the slopes of the 3,142m (10,300ft) **Gunung Agung**. The temple is believed to date to the 14th century and is actually a complex comprising 22 temples. Stepped terraces and stairways ascend to courtyards and gateways, leading up to the main temple building. The Balinese treat Gunung

Gunung Agung eruption

In February 1963, during preparations for the Ekadasa Rudra sacrifice (held once a century), glowing clouds of ash belched from the Gunung Agung volcano. After lying dormant for 120 years, it erupted in March with such violence that the top 100m (330ft) were blown apart. The earth shook, putrid black smoke shot into the air and huge boulders were catapulted out of the centre. Over 1,600 people were killed in the eruption and a further 500 died in the aftermath. The population of the east of the island was threatened by toxic gases, molten lava and colossal rocks. Some 100,000 people were left homeless, and most lost their livelihoods, as entire villages were flattened. Built on a ridge, however, Pura Besakih suffered minor damage.

Pura Besakih *Weaving in Sidemen*

Agung, Bali's highest and holiest mountain, with the greatest respect; they sleep with their heads facing it and the water from its sacred springs is highly sought after for temple rites.

Pura Penataran Agung Besakih

The most important temple here is **Pura Penataran Agung Besakih** with its many multi-roofed *meru* (pagodas). Only worshippers may enter, but visitors can circle the outer walls to glimpse inside and for spectacular views beyond (check out the view from the northeastern end).

Inside the main courtyard are three thrones for the three forms of Shiva, the destroyer. Two other temples symbolise the Hindu trinity: Pura Kiduling Kreteg (Temple South of the Bridge) for Brahma, the creator, and Pura Batu Madeg (Temple of the Upright Stone) for Vishnu, the preserver.

MUNCAN

There are several small restaurants in the car park, but the food is mediocre, so return to the main road instead and drive 2km (1.25 miles) south to **Rendang**. Turn left on a road leading 4km (2.5 miles) east to the old-fashioned village of **Muncan** ❸, alongside the fast-flowing, sacred Telaga Waja River. Monkeys can be seen playing in the trees and the local farmers grow *salak* (snakefruit). Take time to marvel at the spectacular rice terraces, carved into the mountain sides. Further along the road you will see the sign to **Lereng Agung**, see ❶, on the left-hand side.

SIDEMEN

Continue east through Selat, turning right before Duda and then south 10km (6 miles) to the rural, scenic **Sidemen** ❹, which for generations has produced masters of Balinese literature and Hindu theology. The village is also famous for its hand-woven textiles. You can see the weavers at work on their wooden hand-operated looms. You may consider staying at this village; if you do, a pleasant spot for dinner is **Lihat Sawah**, meaning 'rice field view' (see page 102).

Alternatively, continue downhill for about 6km (4 miles) until you reach the junction at the main road. From here you can turn right in the direction of Ubud, or left towards Candidasa.

Food and Drink

❶ LERENG AGUNG RESTORAN

Desa Abuan, Karangasem; daily 10am–6pm; $$

Tour buses stop at this restaurant, where there is an astonishing view incorporating a patchwork of terraced rice fields, river valleys and the volcano. Guests are served an all-you-can-eat (but mediocre) fixed-price Indonesian buffet lunch.

Double-ikat cloth in Tenganan

TENGANAN, CANDIDASA AND AMLAPURA

In the royal Balinese regency of Karangasem, visit an ancient walled stronghold famous for its textiles and bloody ritual battles. Drop by a former palace, wander through two water palaces and travel through breathtaking scenery to laidback Amed.

DISTANCE: 58km (36 miles)
TIME: A full day
START/END: Candidasa/Amed
POINTS TO NOTE: A car, either self-drive or with a driver, is essential for this trip. There is nothing strenuous about it, and it's a fun day out for children with lots of fascinating activities at Tenganan, including watching the buffaloes that wander through the village streets. Later in the day, kids will find plenty of space to run around at Taman Ujung. Bring some cash, because Tenganan is good for handicrafts – don't forget to barter (see page 18). This route is perfect if you are based in Candidasa, and follows on well (on separate days) from the trip around Klungkung and Besakih (route 6).

The island's magnificent eastern regency of Karangasem is an exotic Balinese kingdom of forests and mighty mountains, emerald rice terraces, ancient temples, mystical water palaces and quiet beaches.

Named after an old temple on a nearby hillside, **Candidasa** ❶ is a peaceful seaside destination and a great base from which to visit the regency's many attractions. Notable features include the sacred lotus lagoon just beside the beach and a number of offshore islets and coral reefs, which make for ideal diving and snorkelling. There are numerous hotels and restaurants here.

TENGANAN

After an early breakfast, drive just to the west of Candidasa to a turn-off that heads about 4km (2.5 miles) north (inland) to **Tenganan** ❷, a 700-year-old walled village hidden in the hills (daily 7am–6pm; donation). After signing the visitors' book and paying a small donation at the booth, you enter the village to see stone ramps on three broad parallel avenues running north to south, with narrow lanes running east to west and forming a grid. Tenganan is one of Bali's original pre-Hindu settlements and a stronghold

Bali Aga women preparing for a festival

of native traditions. The residents are the Bali Aga people, descendants of the aboriginal Balinese who resisted the rule of the post-Majapahit kings, fiercely safeguarding their own culture through the conviction that they were descended from the gods. They practise a time-honoured lifestyle based around ritual and ceremony, bound by strict *adat* (customary law) practices to maintain purity.

Council of elders

The buildings in the village have been meticulously positioned in accordance with long-established beliefs. Walking through the village you will see some ceremonial longhouses on your left in the middle of the west lane, including the imposing Bale Agung, where the council of elders makes its decisions. The walled house compounds of the purest descendants line the two sides of this lane; the east lane is for villagers who have married anyone from outside.

Living museum

This fortress-like village has become a living museum, and, as you stroll through the avenues past docile buffaloes with their calves, the villagers may invite you into their houses which also function as shops and workshops, where these expert craftspeople carry out centuries' old skills, including the inscription and decoration of *lontar* palm books, which you will see at the southern end of the village. *Ata* vine basketry is typical of Tenganan, and you will see the baskets woven from this strong vine laid out in the sun to dry at the northern end of the village. Check out the beehives (tiny black bees) and buy some amazing honey from the house in the jungle at the top end of the village. The people are friendly and won't hassle you to buy their products.

Puppet for sale in Tenganan

Shimmering cloths

Tenganan is the only place in Indonesia where the double-*ikat* cloth, known as *kain geringsing* is made. Undyed threads for both weft and warp directions are wound on two separate frames that are the exact length and width of the finished cloth. Charcoal grids are marked on them, and waterproof fibres are tied in complex patterns. The threads are then coloured with natural dyes. This process may be repeated several times, with new sections tied off, while others are opened up. Finally, all the fibres are removed, and the threads are woven. The dyed sections overlap precisely to form exquisite designs, and it can take up to seven years to produce a single piece. The weavers strap themselves into small looms, leaning backwards and forwards to adjust the tension of the threads with their bodies, nudging the threads into position with a pointed twig. The ritually significant cloth is believed to have the power to protect the wearer from sickness and evil. The name may come from the words *gering* (ill) and *sing* (not), although *geringsing* itself means 'speckled', an appropriate description of this shimmering textile.

Village customs

The Bali Aga society is communal, with a distinct social organisation. All of the village property and surrounding fertile farmland belongs to the township as a whole. The villagers do not work the land; instead they lease it to sharecroppers from other villages and receive half the harvest. This leaves the Tenganese free to engage in artistic activities such as weaving, dancing and the music of the *gamelan selonding* (an iron-keyed metallophone), an ancient version of the *gamelan*. They also faithfully adhere to a calendar of complex ceremonies and ritual trance fighting, using prickly *pandanus* leaf whips to draw blood.

Bloody ritual battles

The ritual *mekare-kare* is staged annually in Tenganan in June or July as part of the Usaba Sambah festival. Each duel, which involves the young men of the village fighting each other with prickly *pandanus* leaf whips, takes place to the intense martial sounds of the *gamelan selonding* and lasts only a few seconds, accompanied by much merriment and laughter. The attacks are warded off with tightly woven *ata* vine shields; there are no winners and no losers, because the objective is to draw blood as an offering to the gods. After the battles, the combatants' wounds are treated with a stinging mixture of alcohol and turmeric, leaving no scars.

On the first day of the *mekare-kare* the unmarried maidens of the village ride on creaky wooden ferris wheels, which are manually operated by the men. The turning is supposed to symbolise the descent of the sun to the earth.

Bali Aga women   *Taman Ujung*

AMLAPURA

Drive back to the main road and stop for an early lunch in Candidasa – **Vincent's**, see ❶, is a popular place, as is La Rouge restaurant, see ❷; and the romantic Watergarden, see ❸.

After lunch, continue 20km (12 miles) east over the hills and into **Amlapura** ❸, the largest town in East Bali and the capital of the Karangasem Regency. It used to share the same name as the regency, but in 1963, after the catastrophic eruption of Gunung Agung, the town was 'reborn' as Amlapura to rid itself of any fateful association that villagers were concerned might provoke a much-dreaded recurrence.

Puri Agung Karangasem

The main attraction of Amlapura is the *puri*, or palace, Puri Agung Karangasem. There is a western, a northern, a southern and an eastern *puri*; of these, only the **Puri Kanginan** (Eastern Palace; daily 9am–5pm; charge), on the main road to the market, is easily visited. Follow the one-way streets around the edge of town until you see it on your left.

Enter the front courtyard of the palace to see the Bale Kambang (Floating Pavilion), set in the middle of a large pond. The pavilion was once used by the royal family for relaxation and entertainment.

Located nearby is the European-style Bale Maskerdam, or 'Amster-dam Hall', inside which are housed old photographs, sedan chairs and other royal artefacts. The Maskerdam faces the Bale Pemandesan, or tooth-filing pavilion, which showcases decorative carvings of flowers and animals, executed during the 1920s by Chinese craftsmen.

TAMAN UJUNG

From the centre of Amlapura near the market, head 4km (2.5 miles) south to reach **Taman Ujung** ❹ (daily 8am–6pm; charge). This picturesque pleasure park and water garden was built in 1919 by the last raja of Karangasem, Anak Agung Anglurah Ketut Karangasem. The water palace was formally used from 1921 as a place for the raja to entertain honourable dignitaries, as well as being a retreat for the royal family. It had a vast pool bordered by small pavilions and a European building with stained-glass windows in the centre. Most of the park was destroyed by the 1963 earthquake at the time of the volcanic eruption of Gunung Agung (see page 54), but in 2004 it was completely restored to its former glory. It is a great place for escaping from the heat.

TIRTAGANGGA

Backtrack to Amlapura and take the road northwest in the direction of Abang; after 6km (4 miles) you will see **Tirtagangga** ❺ (daily 9am–5pm admission free) on

Water garden at Taman Ujung

Food and Drink

① VINCENT'S
Jl Raya Canggu; tel: 0363-41368; www.vincentsbali.com; daily 10.30am–late; $$

One of the most popular restaurants in Candidasa, Vincent's offers good-quality international and local cuisine with plenty of vegetarian options. The ambience is friendly and laid back, the garden dining is incredibly romantic, and the artwork indoors is colourful. Lazy jazz music completes the scene.

② LA ROUGE
Jl Raya Candidasa; tel: 0363-41991; daily 10.30am–late; $$

At this luxuriously decorated restaurant, tables spill out into a candlelit garden. The menu is a range of Western, Balinese and Indian food, with lots of seafood and a blackboard of daily specials.

③ WATERGARDEN KAFE
Jl Raya Candidasa; tel: 0363-41540; www.watergardenhotel.com; daily 7am–10.30pm; $$$

The food is reliably good at this romantic, open-air hotel restaurant. The extensive, eclectic menu offers Asian and European cuisine as well as fresh seafood, with classic dishes from Vietnam, Japan, China, Thailand, Morocco and Germany.

your left. This is another royal pleasure park built by the last Raja of Karagasem. The fabled maze of spine-tinglingly cold water pools and basins, spouts, tiered pagoda fountains, moss encrusted statues, stone carvings and lush gardens is a serene and mellow place, showcasing a blend of Chinese and Balinese architectural styles. The neighbouring rice terrace scenery is nothing less than spectacular.

AMED

At the end of the tour you may wish to extend your trip to **Amed** ⑥ on Bali's extreme western tip, and stay for a night or two in this beautiful laid-back area. Continue 10km (6 miles) on the same road northeast, past some dramatic rice terraces and gorgeous scenery to Celuk. Turn right and follow the road 6km (4 miles) to the coast and you will come to a string of fishing villages. Collectively known as Amed, they extend 8km (5 miles) southeast along a spectacular rollercoaster road of steep headlands and dark-sand bays in the shadow of Mt Agung. This coast boasts some of the best coral reefs and dive sites on the island. It is also a great starting point for trekking up the slopes of Gunung Seraya to some of the rarely visited villages. There is a good choice of accommodation in the area, including dive resorts, and numerous rustic beach cafés serving wonderful local cuisine, fresh fish and seafood.

Pura Ulun Danu Bratan

BRATAN AND BEDUGUL

*This action-packed route takes in a market, a lakeside temple and some **beautiful** botanical gardens. It's a fun trip for kids, as they will have a chance **to swing** through the tree-tops or jet-ski **on the lake**.*

DISTANCE: 26km (16 miles)
TIME: A full day
START: Candikuning
END: Munduk
POINTS TO NOTE: This route offers a great day out for families; kids will love posing for photographs with the animals (at Bedugul and on the ridge road above Lake Buyan and Lake Tamblingan), as well as the strawberry treats, the water sports and Treetop Adventure Park. The day includes some strenuous activities, but all of these are optional. A car, either self-drive or with a driver, is essential. While it is possible to get to Bedugul by shuttle bus, with services operating daily from Kuta/Sanur/Ubud, there is only one drop-off point. If you are coming from the south, travel north to Bedugul.

Bali's lake district, set within the vast crater of an ancient, extinct volcano, offers numerous attractions. The refreshing temperature at this high altitude is an average of 10°C (50°F) below the coastal regions, and the views are magnificent, extending across three lakes towards dense rainforests and angular mountains. Make an early start after breakfast, as this is a full day tour.

LAKE BRATAN

Lake Bratan is surrounded by magnificent scenery, with the 2,020m (6,627ft) Gunung Bratan the most prominent feature. The area round the lake is well equipped to cater for visitors.

Candikuning Market
Start the day at **Candikuning ❶**, the main village in the lakeside resort area known as Bedugul, where there are several hotels. Begin by visiting the daily **Bukit Mungsu Market**, a riot of colour and activity. Nowadays it caters largely for visitors, selling handicrafts and souvenirs such as woodcarvings, but it will also give you an insight into some of the locally grown flowers, fruit, vegetables and spices. Make sure you

Muslim schoolchildren, Candikuning

seek out some of the beautiful orchids on sale here.

'Floating' temple

Head down the hill, and the road will bring you alongside the picturesque, alpine-like Danau (Lake) Bratan. About 1km (0.5 miles) from the market, you will see the temple, **Pura Ulun Danu Bratan ❷** (daily 8.30am–6pm; charge), which appears to float on the surface of the water. You'll find images of this temple, often shrouded in mist, on every postcard rack in Kuta.

This large 17th-century Hindu-Buddhist temple complex is set within landscaped gardens. Two multiple-roofed *meru* (pagodas) sit at the edge of Danau Bratan and honour the lake goddess, Dewi Danu, who is the provider of irrigation water for rice fields in the form of bubbling natural springs. The pagodas are not completely surrounded by water, but connected to the shore by narrow strips of land and bamboo bridges, which are erected at the time of temple festivals and ceremonies. A nearby *stupa* (memorial shrine) has four Buddhas in niches around its sides facing the four major compass points. Although entry to the temple itself is not allowed, the surrounding view of the temple complex, beautiful gardens and the majestic but often clouded Gunung Catur is definitely worth seeing.

Strawberry Stop

This cool mountainous area was a favourite place of escape from the heat and humidity for the Dutch colonialists. The climate is perfect for cultivating strawberries, so now might be a good time to taste some of this famous local produce. Take a break at **Strawberry Stop**, see ❶, 200m/yds north of the temple complex on the opposite side

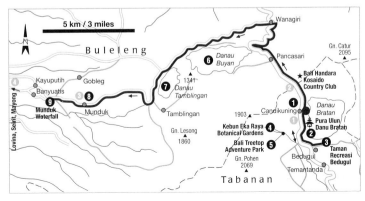

Orchid conservatory at the Botanical Gardens

of the main road, where you can enjoy strawberries served in a variety of ways. You can also have a light lunch here, but for something more substantial you could try **Café Teras**, see ❶, 1.5km (1 mile) further north. This will set you up for an active afternoon, with a choice of water sports on the lake, a tree-top adventure or a stroll through the botanical gardens. Nearby, you will find animal keepers, who will invite you to have your photograph taken with pythons, bats, iguanas, civet cats and hornbills.

Bedugul Recreation Park

If the water looks tempting, **Taman Rekreasi Bedugul** ❸ (Bedugul Recreation Park; daily 8am–6pm; charge), on the southern shores of Lake Bratan offers parasailing, speedboat rental, jet-skiing and water-skiing. Follow the road back up the hill past the market and continue for a further 2km (1.25 miles) until you reach the turning on the left, signposted 'Objek Wisata, Bedugul Water Sports'.

Alternatively, play a round of golf at Bali Handara Kosaido Country Club (tel: 0362-342 2646; www.balihandarakosaido.com), which overlooks Lake Buyan and lays claim to being the only golf course in the world that is nestled inside the caldera of an ancient volcano. It is also listed among the world's top 50 most beautiful courses. The perfectly manicured fairways are complemented by colourful azalea, hibiscus and gladioli and lined by shady mature trees, with a dramatic backdrop of mountains, rainforest, and the peaceful lake.

Botanical Gardens

Alternatively, to the west of the market are **Kebun Eka Raya Botanical Gardens** ❹ (Bedugul Botanical Gardens, Candikuning; daily 8am–6pm; charge). Look out for the statue of the giant corn on the cob, immediately south of the market – the signpost to the gardens is at this junction.

The Botanical Gardens make up a cool, shady park covering 132 hectares (326 acres) of tropical rainforest on the slopes of Gunung Pohon (tree mountain), with over 650 different species of trees and nearly 500 varieties of wild and cultivated orchids; there is even a cactus hothouse.

Treetop Adventure Park

The Botanical Gardens are also home to **Bali Treetop Adventure Park** ❺, (Bedugul Botanical Gardens, Candikuning; daily 8.30am–6pm; last admission 4pm; charge), where you can venture from tree to tree through suspended bridges, spider nets, Tarzan jumps, flying swings and flying foxes. Complying with international safety standards, there are six circuits of varying levels to thrill everyone from small children to adrenaline junkies. Allow 2.5 hours to complete the circuits; the Squirrel Circuits, for children aged 4–8, take 1.5 hours to complete.

Transporting hydrangeas grown in Munduk

LAKE BUYAN AND LAKE TAMBLINGAN

If you want to explore the area a little further, there are some good places for overnight stays (see page 93). Otherwise, follow the main road northwest, up a long, steep winding hill – the walls of the ancient crater. Here, you'll see gregarious grey monkeys frolicking at the road side.

At the top of the hill, turn left along the crater rim road to the two smaller lakes: **Danau Buyan** ❻ (Lake Buyan) and **Danau Tamblingan** ❼ (Lake Tamblingan). These were a single body of water, until a landslide divided them in 1818. Motorboats and water sports are forbidden on these lakes – the natural spring that feeds them provides water for drinking, and the lakes are a rich source of fish, evident by curious wooden, offshore fishing platforms.

MUNDUK

Continue 6km (4 miles) to **Munduk** ❽, a clove- and coffee-growing village overlooking rice terraces, tobacco fields and orange groves. Nearly every gateway here is adorned with pink bougainvillea. Look out for the local people raking and sifting their coffee beans and cloves in courtyards beside the road.

Archaeological evidence indicates that a community was in existence in Munduk from between the 10th and 14th centuries until the Dutch took control of North Bali in the 1890s and turned this area into a cash crop-producing region. Stop for *pisang goreng* (banana fritters) and locally harvested coffee at **Ngiring Ngewedang**, see ❶, perched above the road with spectacular views of palm trees, valleys and jungle stretching to the northwest coast and volcanoes of East Java.

Munduk Waterfall

Below the restaurant, 1km (0.5 miles) along the road, is the 246m (805ft)

Hydrangea harvest

Balinese Hindus believe that their beautiful island is a gift, and for this they pay daily homage by leaving offerings on raised shrines for the attention of the gods and their ancestors, and on the ground to appease demons. These tiny woven palm-frond trays, lined with banana leaf and containing a symbolic assortment of rice, flower petals and incense, are known as *canang*, and the flower most commonly used in these offerings – and cultivated specifically for this purpose – is the blue hydrangea. Hydrangeas, or *pacah seribu*, are grown mainly in the mountainous regions. A visit to the fertile volcanic ridge above lakes Buyan and Tamblingan will reveal boundless fields of the sapphire-tinged flowers stretching to the sea.

Danau Buyan   *Botanical Gardens exhibit*

high **Munduk Waterfall** ❾ (charge). It is well signposted and accessed via steps and a rough, narrow track lined with sweet-smelling clove trees. After a 10-minute walk, you will reach the foot of these majestic falls. This is an alluring place, where you can bathe and absorb the invigorating energy emanating from the cascading water.

The road continues another 16km (10 miles) to Mayong, where it meets the main road to the coast. Turn right and go 10km (6 miles) to Seririt, then turn right again and head 16km (10 miles) to Lovina, where you can base yourself for the night.

In the evening, you may wish to treat yourself by dining at **The Restaurant at Damai Villas**, see ❹, set on the mountain slopes outside Lovina.

Food and Drink

❶ STRAWBERRY STOP

Jl Raya Denpasar-Singaraja, Bedugul; tel: 0362-21060; daily 8am–6pm; $

This simple restaurant is attached to a strawberry farm and serves its home-grown produce in a variety of ways: strawberries whipped into milk shakes, squeezed into juices or stuffed into pancakes with strawberry ice cream and strawberry wine. Also does light meals.

❷ CAFÉ TERAS

Jl Raya Denpasar-Singaraja, Lempuna, Bedugul; tel: 0362-29312; daily 7am–10pm; $$

A Japanese owned cottage restaurant with an air-conditioned, colonial-styled dining room and a pretty garden terrace. Offers a menu of Japanese dishes including miso soup, fusion pasta dishes, salads and teriyaki-style dishes as well as some Indonesian favourites. Alcoholic drinks include *sake*.

❸ NGIRING NGEWEDANG

Munduk, North Bali; www.ngiringngewedang. com; daily 10am–4pm; $

Robusta and Arabica coffee beans from the neighbouring food forests are processed and sold at this enchanting, family-run hill-top restaurant and coffee house (the name means 'please stop by and come in'). Their delicious simple local cuisine includes what are reputedly the best fried noodles and banana fritters on the island.

❹ THE RESTAURANT AT DAMAI VILLAS

Jl Damai, Kayu Putih, Lovina; tel: 0362-41008; www.damai.com; daily 11am–3pm, 7–10pm; $$$$

This celebrated restaurant is located in a boutique retreat nestled on the side of a mountain with views extending to the ocean. Balinese classics are given a gourmet twist, utilising organic produce from the small on-site farm, combined with fresh seafood and imported delicacies. Be sure to make a reservation.

Dolphin-watchers set off from Lovina

LOVINA AND SINGARAJA

This route goes dolphin-watching and explores Bali's old capital of Singaraja, calling in at the world's only library of lontar manuscripts. It also offers a chance to relax at some traditional bathing pools fed by hot springs, before heading further west to Pemuteran, Menjangan and West Bali National Park.

DISTANCE: 90km (56 miles)
TIME: A full day
START/END: Lovina
POINTS TO NOTE: For this route, you should base yourself on the north coast, in Lovina (ideally in the village of Kalibukbuk), as it begins with a 5.45am pick-up from your hotel by your boat captain. The route can be done in one day, or it can be cut into two one-day tours. If time permits, the second half of this itinerary can be tagged on to route 8.

The peaceful atmosphere, calm seas and palm-fringed, dark-sand beaches of north Bali have been attracting adventurous young travellers since the 1970s.

LOVINA

Lovina ❶ – actually a long string of coastal villages (Pemaron, Tukad Mungga, Anturan, Kalibukbuk, Kaliasem and Temukus) to the west of **Singaraja** – is an excellent base for exploring the north coast, as there are plenty of hotels and restaurants here. The liveliest vil-

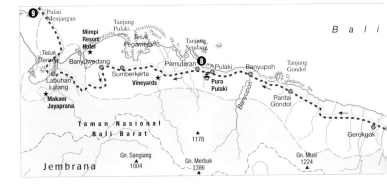

Brahma Arama Vihara

lage is **Kalibukbuk** ❷. Lovina was given its name in the 1960s by the last king of Buleleng, who purchased a small tract of land in Kaliasem and built the Tasik Madu (Sea of Honey) Hotel. It is possible that the name was chosen to signify the love in the hearts of the people, or it may refer to a pair of Santen trees that the king planted which grew to embrace each other.

Dolphin trips

Lovina Bay has a pretty black volcanic-sand beach fringed by coconut palms against a backdrop of hills; the sea here is great for swimming. Lovina is famous for the spotted, spinner and bottlenose dolphins that gather in large schools within the bay; note the dolphin statue beside the beach. A memorable activity is to go on an early morning **dolphin-watching excursion** (daily 6am; charge). There's no need to look for a tour operator, as all the boats offer the same trip for the same price; you will need to make arrangements the night before at your hotel and be ready at 5.45am (the boatman may knock on your door to wake you up) for the ride in a motorised traditional *jukung* fishing boat. About 90 percent of trips have successful sightings.

Return to Kalibukbuk for breakfast. **Café Made**, see ❶, is a good inexpensive option.

SINGARAJA

After breakfast, head 10km (6 miles) east by car to **Singaraja** ❸ – the name means 'Lion King', commemorating a palace built in 1604 by Raja Panji Sakti. For hundreds of years Chinese, Indian and Arab traders brought their products, religion and culture through this trade port, which was Bali's capital from 1855 until the Dutch moved it south to Denpasar after defeating the royal families there in 1906.

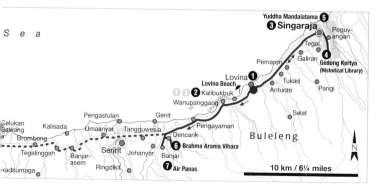

Statue at Brahma Arama Vihara

The city still has some good examples of colonial architecture and is a major educational and cultural centre of present-day Bali.

Gedong Kertya

Stop by **Gedong Kertya** ❹ (23 Jalan Veteran; Mon–Thur 8am–3.30pm, Fri 8am–1pm; free), at the southern end of town. This library was founded in 1928 by the ruler of Buleleng, I Gusti Putu Djlantik, and the resident (government official during Dutch rule) of Bali and Lombok, LJJ Caron, who recognised the need to collect, copy and preserve thousands of *lontar* manuscripts.

The manuscripts cover subjects such as astronomy, ritual ceremonies, rules and regulations, religion, Balinese architecture, Balinese philosophy, genealogy, homeopathy, *usada* (medical manuscripts), history of the Hindu kingdom, folklore and black magic. Dried fan leaves from the *rontal* palm are inscribed with a pointed stylus and wiped with oily burnt macadamia nuts to make the lines visible. Many also have fine illustrations.

Old harbour

From here, head 3km (2 miles) down Jl Gajah Mada towards the old harbour. Most of the original structures on the waterfront were destroyed by high waves in the early 1990s, but there are still a few Dutch-style buildings and a Chinese *klenteng* (temple) by the shore. The Chinese were once very active as traders in Singaraja.

Look out for the monument of a soldier bearing a flag, jutting out over the water's edge. This is **Yuddha Mandalatama** ❺, commemorating the Indonesian struggle for independence against the Dutch from 1945 to 1949.

Lunch in Lovina

At this point, head back to Lovina for lunch. There are lots of cheap and cheerful restaurants on the two parallel streets that run down to the beach in Kalibukbuk. **Kakatua**, see ❷, has a huge menu.

BRAHMA ARAMA VIHARA

From Lovina, drive 8km (5 miles) west along the main road. At Dencarik turn inland (south) 1.5km (1 mile) to **Banjar** and follow the sign to the **Brahma Arama Vihara** ❻ (daily 8am–6pm, closed 10 days in Apr and Sept; free), a Buddhist monastery located 2km (1.25 miles) up a hillside. Dress respectfully, speak softly and remove your shoes before entering.

AIR PANAS HOT SPRINGS

Follow the narrow road further to **Air Panas** ❼ (daily 9am–6pm; charge), a natural hot spring set in a landscaped environment. In 1985, the 38°C (100°F) sulphuric waters, which are believed to cure skin ailments, were channelled to pour out of carved serpent spouts into a set of traditional bathing pools, one of which is fed by 3m (10ft) high spouts to give a pummelling massage.

The Buddhist monastery   *Air Panas hot springs*

PEMUTERAN

Backtrack to the main road and either return to Lovina or turn left continuing 44 km (27 miles) west to **Pemuteran** ❶, where you may wish to stay as the accommodation is more upmarket than in Lovina. The black-sand beach here leads to an excellent dive site, or you can enjoy a trek inland through thick lowland forest bordered by towering mountains. There is also a pearl farm where you can buy jewellery. The nearby village of Perancak is the home of a small community-run turtle conservation programme, and for a small donation you can sponsor the release of these endangered creatures into the sea.

MENJANGAN

Ten km (6 miles) further west along the main road will bring you to Labuhan Lalang, the jump-off point for the tiny uninhabited **Menjangan Island** ❾, which is located within the boundaries of the West Bali National Park. The excellent coral reefs surrounding the island offer some of Bali's best snorkelling and dive sites. Boats can be chartered from the Labuhan Lalang visitors' centre, along with snorkelling equipment. Dive trips are better arranged from Pemuteran.

WEST BALI NATIONAL PARK

If you wish to go hiking in the National Park, you can obtain the necessary permits at the visitor centre in Labuhan Lalang (7.30am–5pm); an official guide is compulsory as visitors are not allowed to trek on their own. Established in 1984, the 760 square kilometres of forested mountains, coasts and offshore reefs are the last remaining pristine areas on the island. This is a birdwatchers paradise and home to deer, civets, monkeys, the rare wild Javan buffalo, and the nearly extinct Bali Starling.

Food and Drink

❶ CAFÉ MADE

Jl Ketapang, Kalibukbuk; tel: 081-337-422247; daily 8am–11pm; $

Located at the beach end of Jl Ketapang, 500m/yds from the dolphin statue, Café Made is open at the front, with views over the street. Inside, there are colourful artworks on the walls. It serves sandwiches, snacks, international favourites, classic Balinese and Indonesian dishes and fresh fish.

❷ KAKATUA BAR & RESTAURANT

Jl Pantai Binaria, Kalibukbuk; tel: 0362-41344/41144; daily 8am–11pm; $

At Kakatua, two open-sided pavilions are linked by a fish pond and pots of flowering plants. The delicious hearty fare from the simple open kitchen ranges from pizza, pasta and cauliflower cheese to Indian curries, Mexican fare, Thai dishes and home-made puddings.

Door detail, Krambitan palace

KRAMBITAN, PUPUAN AND MEDEWI

Visit two palaces at a royal town before heading into the mountains past clove and coffee plantations and rice terraces. Drive through a giant tree and watch the sunset from a remote surf beach on the splendid west-facing coast.

DISTANCE: 86km (53 miles)
TIME: A full day
START: Krambitan
END: Medewi
POINTS TO NOTE: This route in the Tabanan Regency involves a lot of driving on mountain roads, so will be less tiring if you arrange for a car and driver rather than self-drive. It links well with route 11.

Once a powerful kingdom, the rural region of Tabanan now incorporates vast expanses of terraced rice fields, royal palaces and historically important villages that function as centres for traditional music and dance.

KRAMBITAN

This route begins at the royal town of **Krambitan ❶**, which is 9km (5.5 miles) southwest of the city of Tabanan. Krambitan has two palaces belonging to a branch of the Tabanan royal family: the older **Puri Gede** and the newer **Puri Anyar**, both with beautiful architecture. The royal household here has a fine private collection of *lontar* manuscripts (see page 68). Since 1972, 'Palace Nights' have been held for tourists at Puri Anyar. These involve a performance of a *tektekan* by an ensemble from nearby Panarukan. The *tektekan* is an exciting rendition of the dramatic Calonarang exorcist trance drama performed to the rhythmic beating of bamboo slit drums, which produce a 'tek' sound when struck. *Tektekan* was traditionally used to chase away malevolent spirits that were responsible for bringing disaster, such as drought or pestilence, to a village. Artists in Krambitan have also created a uniquely local style of *wayang* (puppet figure) painting – a traditional art in which the *wayang* puppet figures are depicted in paintings.

SCENIC DRIVE

From Krambitan, go northwest 5km (3 miles) back to the main road at Melil-

The Bunut Bolong tree

ing. Turn left and drive 10km (6 miles) west to **Antosari**, then turn right and begin a scenic drive up the mountains towards Pupuan. There are two options for lunch en route; the first one is after about 12km (7 miles) in the village of **Belimbing ❷** (the name means starfruit). Here you will find the remote **Café Belimbing**, see ❶, set high above the road with spectacular panoramic views. Alternatively, continue another 9km (5.5 miles) to **Sanda ❸** and stop for a feast at **Plantations**, see page 103, at Sanda Butik Villas. The awesome view from this restaurant, which is located 700m (2,300ft) above sea level, takes in a vast wooded valley and rice terraces as far as the eye can see.

CLOVE PLANTATIONS

Continue north for another 8km (5 miles) to **Pupuan** and then turn left off the main road, heading first west and then south and downhill on a winding road. After 19km (12 miles) you will reach the isolated mountain village of **Tista** (not to be confused with the trance dance village of Tista near Krambitan). Take the road signposted to the village of **Asahduren ❹**, and 10km (6 miles) will bring you to the clove plantations – trim spice trees with orange tipped leaves. You might see and smell the fragrant flower buds drying on mats beside the road. Plantations of coffee and cocoa are also grown in this area of mountains and rainforest.

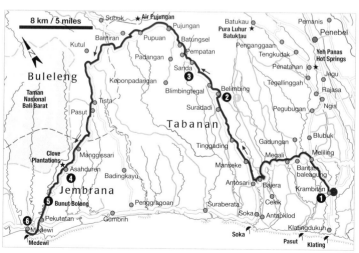

Belimbing rice terraces

BUNUT BOLONG

From here, it's 11km (7 miles) down to the coast. Along the way, you will drive through **Bunut Bolong** ❺, a gigantic *bunut*, a type of banyan tree, with the road going through its trunk. Banyan trees continually sprout long aerial roots that grow down the trunk or dangle from a branch. Once the roots reach the ground, they enlarge to form new trunks. The banyan tree is known as the 'tree that walks' because it moves forward with every new trunk it puts out.

These massive banyan trees are a common sight in Bali – as you travel around, you will see them towering above almost every village temple and cemetery. Not only are they considered to be the 'elders' of the tree kingdom, it is believed that they are inhabited by spirits and demons, hence they are accorded special respect. They are carefully preserved and worshipped, and the Balinese build shrines at their feet, girding their trunks with the black-and-white chequered *poleng* cloth that marks the sacred. You may notice that motorists will honk their horns in polite greeting if they pass a banyan tree on the road. These majestic trees can grow to over 30m (100ft) in height and display a refreshing canopy of green above their multiple trunks.

A shrine guarded by colourful tiger figures has been built next to Bunut Bolong for the wayward local spirits to reside in. Just beyond the tree is a viewpoint with a splendid outlook over the expansive, forested mountains of western Bali.

MEDEWI

On the coastal route, continue 2km (1.25 miles) westwards to the dark-sand beach of **Medewi** ❻, where you can watch surfers catching the last breaks while the sun sets. It's not a good idea to swim here, though, as the waves can be huge, and the currents are very strong.

If you wish to spend some more time on this stretch of coast, take the main road east 16km (10 miles) to Balian – another popular surf spot named after the river estuary here – and stay at the enchanting **Gajah Mina Resort** on the headland. At the very least, stop for dinner at **Naga** (see page 103), the hotel's romantic restaurant, where you can sample delectable, healthy, fresh cuisine, much of it made with their home-grown produce.

Food and Drink

① CAFÉ BELIMBING (STARFRUIT CAFÉ)

Banjar Suradadi; daily 8am–9pm; no tel; $

This delightful, simple open-air café has panoramic views over rice terraces, coffee and clove plantations and an extensive menu as well as daily specials. The high-quality Indonesian and Western food includes healthy salads, snacks, pastas, wicked puddings and fresh fruit juices.

Pura Tanah Lot

TANAH LOT, JATILUWIH AND BATUKAU

Begin with a Balinese blessing at a wave-lashed sea temple, then take in the magnificent views as you drive up the slopes of Gunung Batukau, Bali's second-highest peak, to a mountain temple. End at Yeh Panas hot springs.

DISTANCE: 73km (45 miles)
TIME: A full day
START: Pura Tanah Lot
END: Yeh Panas
POINTS TO NOTE: This route involves a lot of driving, so will be less tiring if you arrange for a car and driver rather than self-drive especially as the roads are quite steep and twisting. Take extra caution during the rainy season (Nov–Mar). This route is ideal if you are staying in the Seminyak or Canggu area. Alternatively, it can follow on from the Krambitan, Pupuan and Medewi trip (route 10), in which case it should be done in reverse.

The Tabanan Regency presents rice fields stretching from the coast up to an altitude of 700m (2,300ft). It is also home to Gunung Batukau, which, at 2,276m (7,467ft) above sea level, is the second-highest peak in Bali. It is known as the 'Stone Coconut Shell Mountain' thanks to its inverted *kau* or *karu* (coconut shell) profile.

The Tabanan Regency is known as Bali's 'rice bowl' and is the most agriculturally productive region on the island, yielding not only rice but coffee, cacao, palm-sugar, vanilla, candlenut, cloves and tropical fruits such as durian, jackfruit, mangosteen, *salak* (snakefruit), coconuts and avocados. Meanwhile the area around Mt Batukau has the greatest biological diversity in Bali. Wildlife endemic to this area includes the small forest deer known as *kijang*, the rare, black, leaf-eating monkey, the *landak* (porcupine), the *lubak* (mongoose), flying lizards and beautiful butterflies and moths.

Start early for this long, scenic trip. If you are staying in the south or the Ubud area, first drive to **Kerobokan** and then take the road 16km (10 miles) west to **Tanah Lot**, which is well signposted all the way. If you are staying in the Canggu area, you will see the signs on the main road directing you towards Tanah Lot. Visiting the temple of Pura Tanah Lot at this early hour means that you will be avoiding the busloads of tourists that almost always arrive before sunset.

Delicate flora at Pura Luhur Batukau

PURA TANAH LOT

Pura Tanah Lot ❶ (daily 7am–7pm; charge includes parking), the small 'Temple of the Land in the Sea', rests offshore on a rocky outcrop that becomes encircled by water at high tide. Scores of souvenir stalls line the pathway down to the beach, while rows of cafés occupy the cliff opposite the temple, together with a small stall selling *kopi luwak* – civet cat coffee. There are some tame civet cats here that you can stroke.

Pura Tanah Lot is one of the most important sea temples in Bali, and people from all over the island come here to pray, especially during the temple's *odilan* (anniversary festival). The temple was built in the 16th century by the legendary Hindu priest, Danghyang Nirartha, who left his home in Java as its population was converting to Islam. When he arrived in Bali, he is said to have followed a strange glow emanating from this spot, its natural beauty inspiring him to spend the night in meditation. When local inhabitants bothered him, he moved the land he was on out into the sea, thus giving it its name.

Holy snakes

When Danghyang Nirartha departed, he instructed the people to build a temple here to commemorate his visit. He left behind his sash, which turned into poisonous sea snakes. These snakes are to be found living in caves and rocks around the base of the outcropping, and are said to guard the temple against intruders. You will be invited over to a cave on the mainland side to view (and even touch) one of these holy snakes, which will be coiled up asleep. In return for a nominal donation, the duty *pemanku* (lay priest) will illuminate the snake for you with his torch.

Hindu blessing

At low tide, walk across the sand to a cave below the temple and receive a Balinese Hindu blessing from a priest in exchange for a donation. You will be asked to make a wish as you cup your hands and receive some holy water to ritually wash your face; the priest will then place some dried rice on your forehead – remember to leave this in place until it drops off. If this doesn't appeal, you can admire the view from the beach.

PURA ALAS KEDATON

Leave Tanah Lot and head inland (north) through **Beraban** on a road that winds 9km (5.5 miles) through rice fields and small villages to **Kediri**. Drive north another 5km (3 miles) and turn right onto a road that takes you a short way east to **Pura Alas Kedaton** ❷ (daily 7am–6pm; charge).

Known as the 'Temple of the Royal Forest', the temple complex has monkeys and fruit bats living in the surrounding trees. The walk through the

Jatiluwih rice terraces   *Working on the rice terraces*

forest is more interesting than the renovated Pura Dalem, or 'Temple of the Dead', which you cannot enter. Guides will show you around for a small fee.

Backtrack to the main road and go 2km (1.25 miles) uphill before turning right at **Peken** and travelling the same distance south to **Belayu ❸**, where you can buy fine *songket* textiles, combined with gold thread and hand-woven by the village women.

PACUNG

Return to Peken and travel east for another 1km (0.5 miles) before turning left onto the good paved main road leading 24km (15 miles) uphill to **Pacung**. Stop at **Pacung Indah Hotel**, see ❶, and enjoy a buffet lunch looking across magnificent rice terraces to the east, with the sacred mountain, Gunung Agung, as a backdrop when the weather is clear.

JATILUWIH

The best is yet to come. Take the narrow winding road 13km (8 miles) west through steep rice terraces to **Jatiluwih ❹**, a Unesco World Heritage Site since 2008 for its preservation of traditional Balinese farming techniques. True to its name – 'extraordinary' or 'truly marvellous' – this scenic point at a height of 850m (2,700ft) above sea level offers one of the most breathtaking panoramic views imaginable. There are several restaurants here where you can stop for refreshments. The rich pattern made by the banana plantations and newly planted rice are reminiscent of a complex batik.

Riding through Jatiluwih's terraces

PURA LUHUR BATUKAU

Continue along the road for 4km (2.5 miles) to **Wongayagede**, and turn right on the main road for another 2km (1.25 miles) to **Pura Luhur Batukau** ❺ (daily 8am–5pm; charge). This 'Lofty Stone Coconut Shell Temple' complex, which venerates the deities of mountains and lakes, is located about halfway up the mountain slopes of Gunung Batukau.

It was the ancestral temple for the royal family of Tabanan, whose descendants still maintain the shrines. Two smaller temples, Pura Dalem and Pura Pan-yaum, are found on the lower level.

On the eastern side is an artificial pond with two shrines in the middle. One is dedicated to the goddess of Danau Tamblingan (see page 64), while the other is for the god of Gunung Batukau, thus representing the concept of *rwa bhineda* (cosmic duality), the Balinese equivalent of Chinese yin-yang philosophy.

YEH PANAS HOT SPRINGS

Descend 8km (5 miles) back down the main road to **Penatahan**, for a soak in the sulphurous hot springs at **Yeh Panas** ❻ (daily 7am–7pm; tel: 0361-854 0851). Such natural phenomena as hot springs are believed in Bali to be frequented by spirits, so Yeh Panas has a small temple, where people make offerings with prayers. The springs have been turned into a simple spa at a small hotel, which non-residents may use for a fee; there are nine private and semi-private pools.

Afterwards, take the left turn-off going southeast for 4km (2.5 miles), until it joins the main road heading 10km (6 miles) south through Wanasari and all the way down to Tabanan. From here it's an easy 13km (8 mile) drive to Sempidi, where major roads lead back to the main tourist centres. You could stop for dinner at **The Beach House**, see ❷.

Food and Drink

❶ PACUNG INDAH HOTEL & RESTAURANT

Pacung; tel: 0368-21020; www.pacung bali.com; daily 7am–9pm; $$

The restaurant at this hillside hotel, blessed with beautiful views, serves a daily Indonesian buffet lunch as well as *à la carte* meals. The focus is on local cuisine, but Western dishes are also available.

❷ THE BEACH HOUSE

Jl Pura Batu Mejan (Echo Beach), Canggu; tel: 0361-738471; www.echobeachhouse. com; daily 8am–11pm; $$

This popular restaurant has tables spilling out onto a beach-side bluff – a great place to watch the sunset. The international menu includes Indonesian dishes, and there is a daily barbecue of seafood. Friendly staff, potent Martinis and live music on Sunday evenings.

View of Mount Agung from Mushroom Bay

NUSA LEMBONGAN, NUSA CENINGAN AND NUSA PENIDA

Make a getaway to three nearby islands for water sports and time out on the beach. Explore the mangrove forest in a canoe, visit an underground cave house, and head for a temple associated with black magic.

DISTANCE: On Nusa Lembongan and Nusa Ceningan 17km (10.5 miles); on Nusa Penida 38km (23 miles)
TIME: A day, or two days if you wish to visit Nusa Penida
START/END: Nusa Lembongan
POINTS TO NOTE: If snorkelling and water sports are all you have in mind, book yourself on a day trip (Bali Hai Cruises; tel: 0361-720331; www.balihaicruises.com). These offshore islands are accessible on pleasure cruises or a fast boat leaving from Sanur (a reliable operator is Scoot Fast Cruises, www.scootcruise.com). If you go by cheaper public boats, the crossing can be rough, slow and even dangerous depending on sea conditions. You can also charter your own vessel, but this may end up riskier than a commercial cruise.

Nusa Lembongan, the tiny, sparsely populated **Nusa Ceningan** and **Nusa Penida** are a trio of islands located 20km (12 miles) off Bali's east coast – just 30 to 60 minutes' cruise by boat from **Benoa Harbour**. Steeped in tradition, village life on Nusa Lembongan is slow and enchanting, and this is where most of the pleasure boats take visitors on packaged day tours. If you want to stay for a few days, there are alternative options for independent travellers.

NUSA LEMBONGAN

Arriving at **Nusa Lembongan ❶**, boats dock at Mushroom Bay and Jungut Batu. Despite its tiny size, the island offers lots of activities ranging from fishing, kayaking, diving and surfing to cycling, visiting the seaweed farms, or exploring the mangrove forest in a dugout canoe. There are plenty of water sport facilities, and restaurants range from barefoot beach bars to fine dining at **Jojo's Restaurant**, see ❶.

Nusa Lembongan's white-sand beaches are fringed by a beautiful reef which supports its own ecosystem and has been declared a protected marine park as it contains large expanses of coral gardens. The majority of visitors

Seaweed farmers' houses near Jungut Batu

swim, snorkel and nap for most of the day, as the weather can get very hot and dry. Crystal-clear waters in an idyllic bay make for excellent snorkelling and scuba diving; the former from offshore pontoons or drifting charter boats, the latter with one of the PADI dive operators on the island, such as World Diving Lembongan (Pondok Baruna Guesthouse, Jungut Batu; tel: 081-239-00686; www.world-diving.com). The waters around Nusa Penida and Nusa Lembongan are frequented by migratory sunfish in October.

Dream Beach

If you're not into water sports, since the roads are generally well surfaced you could consider hiring a motorcycle (which any of the cafés at Mushroom Bay or Jungut Batu can arrange) and heading over to clearly signposted **Dream Beach**, on the south coast. The journey takes about 15 minutes. On the way, stop on the cliff top for a photo opportunity at **Devil's Tear ❷**, a rocky outcrop where the dramatic crashing of waves creates water plumes and high-pressure spouts. Just south of here is Dream Beach, a gorgeous spot with an often-deserted beach of powdery white sand. Swimming can be dangerous though, as the current can be very strong. Try **Café Pandan** at Dream Beach Huts, see ❷, for a casual lunch and make use of the infinity-edge swimming pool overlooking the beach.

Jungut Batu

Alternatively, if time allows, a 30-minute or so walk from Mushroom Bay takes you to the main village of **Jungut Batu ❸**, with its sandy compounds and squat pavilions surrounded by thick and low coral or limestone walls. From here, take the beach road north and turn into the mangroves. Continue for 1.5km (1 mile) to the Robinson Crusoe-style **Mangrove Stop Restaurant**, see ❶, positioned at the eastern end of the spit of land that runs through the northern mangrove forest. You can also get there by boat from Mushroom Bay – any boat captain will know the way. Once there you can go on a delightful gondola-type boat ride through the shady mangroves, but be sure to bargain hard for a reasonable price, say Rp50,000-100,000, before you set out.

Continue on foot 1km (0.5 miles) further south to **Lembongan ❹**, a fishing village where the local people farm seaweed within a patchwork of underwater, bamboo-fenced plots. Seaweed farming on the three islands is labour intensive and time consuming. Women are the main labourers, and growth is so fast that new shoots can be harvested every 45 days. The produce is then dried and exported, mainly to Japan, for processing and use in cosmetics. Most of the day cruises run by Bali Hai (see page 77) include a tour of the seaweed farm and village on Nusa Ceningan.

Along the way, pause on the hilltop where, on a clear day, there are stun-

Drying seaweed   *Sunset over Mushroom Bay*

ning views across Badung Strait to Bali. Birdwatchers should look out for flashes of white and turquoise denoting the sacred kingfisher (like the collared kingfisher but slightly smaller and common to this island). Nusa Lembongan's white-sand beaches are fringed by a beautiful reef, which supports its own eco-system and has been declared a protected marine park containing large expanses of coral gardens.

Rumah di Bawah Tanah

At Jungut Batu on the south side of the hill, visit the cave house known as

Rumah di Bawah Tanah (donation to the late priest's family), a bizarre underground house built over 50 years ago by a local priest acting on divine inspiration. The multiple tunnels, nooks and crannies carved out from limestone can be rather eerie.

NUSA CENINGAN

Follow the coast from the end of Jungut Batu beach, past Mushroom Bay to the Ceningan Strait on the east side of the island. This is a 3km (2-mile) walk. Alternatively, if you have hired a

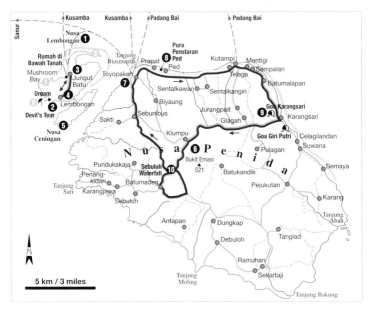

Pura Segara, part of the Penataran Ped temple complex

motorcycle, just follow the main road from the cave house in order to then cross on foot to the tiniest of the three islands, **Nusa Ceningan** ❺ (the name means small island) by means of a scenic suspension bridge. In March 2013 the bridge collapsed in high winds but is expected to be rebuilt; alternatively you can charter a boat. The island is home to a small village of seaweed farmers, whose boats you will see crowded around their plantations in the late afternoons. Return to your lodgings or boat before sunset as the paths are not lit at night.

NUSA PENIDA

If you are staying overnight on Nusa Lembongan, charter a boat (from Mushroom Bay or Jungut Batu) to take you early next morning to Toyopakeh, on the island of **Nusa Penida** ❻. This is the largest of the three islands, measuring approximately 200 sq km (77 sq miles), with towering limestone sea cliffs. There is little infrastructure and not many facilities for tourists, just a few *losmen* (family-run guesthouses) and a number of small *warungs* (roadside cafés).

During the 18th and 19th centuries, Nusa Penida was a penal colony for the Klungkung Kingdom, which meant that criminals, undesirables and political agitators were sent here after having been judged in the Kerta Gosa (see page 53). In spite of these dubious roots, the people are quite friendly and welcome visitors to their remote 'Limestone Island'. Nusa Penida is famous for its *kain cepuk*, a hand-woven *ikat* (weft tie-dyed) cloth with complex, multicoloured geometric patterns on a red or maroon background. Powerful magical properties are attributed to this textile, which is worn by Rangda, the widow-witch of Balinese exorcist drama.

Life is hard on Nusa Penida, with the locals making a living from fishing and farming, with seaweed probably the largest export. Few opportunities exist for education and employment.

Pura Dalem Ped

Settlers from Java, Lombok and Sulawesi are also to be found in the main town of **Toyopakeh** ❼. Pack lunch or snacks and lots of bottled water. When you boat arrives in Toyopakeh, you will be greeted by *angot* (public transportation) drivers who will invite you to rent their car (including driver and petrol). The price is negotiable but Rp 200,000 seems to be the going rate for five hours.

First head 3km (2 miles) east to the **Penataran Ped** complex and **Pura** ❽ (donation), the most important temple in the Bali Province for practitioners of black magic. Worshippers from all over Bali come here to pray during its *odilan*, or temple anniversary festival, which occurs once every 210 days. Everything is decorated with *poleng* (black-and-

Crystal Bay, Nusa Penida

Seaweed cultivation, Toyopakeh harbour

white chequered cloths), symbolic of negative and positive cosmic forces.

Always ask permission from the priests before entering, and don't forget to leave a small donation. Growing inside is a strange tangle of three different trees forming a great twisted mass and the atmosphere is rather spooky – as befits the temple's reputation. The patron deity here is Ratu Gede Mas Mecaling, the 'Fanged Lord of Victims', who, along with his invisible henchmen in the guise of fireballs, flies to Bali, landing on the beach at Lebih to spread disease and pestilence during the rainy season. The Balinese repel them with the lord's own fearsome image in the *barong landung* (tall puppet figures) of Jero Gede and his wife, Jero Luh, with their smiling faces.

Several other places on the island are worth visiting. Drive 10km (6 miles) along the northeast coast to see the enormous limestone cavern of **Goa Karangsari** ❾, with two shrines set in a grotto. The entrance lies 150m (492ft) up a steep stairway. Some of the branch tunnels lead to openings from where there are breathtaking views.

Continue south up into the hills, then northwest for 16km (10 miles) to **Sebuluh Waterfall** ❿ near **Batumadeg**, an unusual sight in such a dry place but really only impressive during the rainy season.

Finally, head north, back to Toyapakeh before sunset for a boat to Lembongan, or return to Bali.

Food and Drink

❶ JOJO'S RESTAURANT

Nusa Lembongan Resort, Mushroom Bay, Nusa Lembongan; tel: 0361-725864; www.nusalembonganresort.com; daily 7am–10pm; $$$

This upmarket resort restaurant is an open pavilion idyllically positioned to overlook the beach edging the coral bay. The menu offers a wide selection of Indonesian and international dishes, including plenty of fresh seafood.

❷ CAFÉ PANDAN

Dream Beach Huts, Nusa Lembongan; www.dreambeachlembongan.com; tel: 081-338-737344; daily 7am–10pm; $$

This open-air café and bar overlooks the stunning Dream Beach and offers a great selection of Balinese, Thai and Western dishes as well as a huge list of cocktails, which can be consumed in the café, beside the pool, or on sunbeds on a low bluff above the beach.

❸ MANGROVE STOP RESTAURANT

Mangrove Point, Nusa Lembongan; daily 11am–9pm; $$

This rustic Robinson Crusoe-style restaurant is both romantic and close to nature. Set within the cool shady mangroves, it serves classic Indonesian delights as well as a selection of simple Western dishes.

DIRECTORY

Hand-picked hotels and restaurants to suit all budgets and tastes, organised by area, plus select nightlife listings, an alphabetical listing of practical information, a language guide and an overview of the best books and films to give you a flavour of the island.

Accommodation	84
Restaurants	94
Nightlife	104
A–Z	106
Language	118
Books and Film	120

Palm trees on Bali's southeast coast

ACCOMMODATION

Bali has a very wide range of accommodation, from over-the-top luxury hotels to cheap family-run guesthouses (also known as *losmen*). Most top-end hotels in Kuta, Jimbaran, Sanur and Nusa Dua are located on the beach and are of international standards. Many places have slightly higher rates during the peak tourist season from July to August, and from mid-December to mid-January. Reservations are recommended for the larger hotels during these peak periods. In the low season negotiate for lower rates. Deluxe and luxury accommodation will include hot water, air conditioning, and usually IDD telephone and other facilities. Budget and economy places often include a simple breakfast.

Alternatives to staying in a hotel include renting fully serviced apartments, or renting a private villa. Many wealthy foreigners and Indonesians from Jakarta have built luxury homes in Bali which they hire out to visitors on a daily or weekly basis. A villa can be anything from a 1-bedroom beachside cottage to an exclusive 8-bedroom luxury villa with every conceivable comfort. Nearly every private villa has a swimming pool and the majority accommodate between two and 10 people and come equipped with kitchen and dining facilities, plus a complement of staff, from housekeepers and cooks to drivers, gardeners, pool attendants and security guards. The Villa Guide (www.thevillaguide.com), a villa-management agency based in Bali, has a sterling reputation.

South Bali: There's no real reason to stay in **Denpasar** unless you have urgent business that can't wait the short (15-minute) commute from Kuta. There are scores of hotels for under US$20, most of them catering to domestic tourists.

Kuta is chaotic and noisy but a great playground. Years of unplanned development have turned it into a jumble of loosely packed pubs, nightclubs, restaurants, shops and budget hotels. Even with many first-class hotels, the area still caters best to the economy traveller who likes to be in the thick of things. The northern end of Kuta beach is known as **Legian**, a little quieter and more relaxed than teeming Kuta.

Seminyak lies to the north of Legian. It has the same sweeping beach and surf as Kuta and Legian but not the pressing crowds and vendors. The area has several luxury and mid-price hotels but scant budget places. Nearby Jalan Laksmana

Price for a double room (subject to a 10–21 percent tax and service charge):
$$$$ = over US$200
$$$ = US$120–200
$$ = US$60–120
$ = below US$60

Welcoming butler

Idyllic coastal hotel grounds

heaves with restaurants while Jalan Raya Seminyak has upmarket shops.

Jimbaran, south of Kuta and the airport, is a sweeping bay that curves for 5km (3 miles) to the headland. There are a handful of luxury resorts and the beach remains unspoilt and tranquil. A string of beachside seafood restaurants at Jimbaran provide alternatives to hotel food.

The Bukit is the rugged limestone peninsula that dangles like a pendant upon a chain at the southern tip of Bali. Until recently, this remote windswept outcrop was home solely to seaweed farmers, fishermen and die-hard surfers. It has now reinvented itself to become the most upmarket destination on the island.

A destination for foreigners since the 1920s, **Sanur** offers peace and quiet. It has an 'international' ambience but is far less cosmopolitan than frenetic Kuta, and has both first-class and budget hotels.

Nusa Dua is rather isolated from the rest of Bali, but is blessed with fine white-sand beaches. To make up for the area's somewhat sterile character, hotels here provide everything on the premises. A few restaurants line the road outside the hotel area. The northern end of Nusa Dua is a long finger-shaped peninsula with a white sand beach that is lined with upmarket hotels and water sports operations. Its waters can be as still as a mill pond at low tide because of the protective coral reef offshore.

There are many mid-range and budget hotels in the centre of **Ubud**, all within walking distance of markets, art galleries, shops and restaurants.

East Bali: Don't expect much of a beach at **Candidasa**: coral dredged from the sea over the years has led to serious erosion. There are isolated patches of sand but a number of hotels have got around this by buildings over the water. There is not much choice on **Nusa Lembongan** but the best hotels are situated on Mushroom Bay.

North Bali: Most hotels in the **Lovina** area have a stretch of black-sand beach. There is no surf as the beach as protected by the distant reef, so it is very safe for young children. Set within the crater of an extinct volcano, the **Bedugul area** consists of a small market town, spectacular golf course and three lakes, providing a flavour of rural Bali.

Tabanan region: The coast area is relatively sparse with good accommodation. Most of the area's attractions are undertaken as day trips from Ubud or Kuta.

Kuta/Legian

Casa Padma Suites

Jl Padma, Legian; tel: 0361-753073; www.casapadmasuites.com; $$

This small boutique hotel is built around the elongated swimming pool and The Drops restaurant extends out over it. A mix of six standard rooms and 23 suites, some of which have their own terraces, it is close to restaurants, bars, shops and the beach.

Lace bedding in Seminyak

Hard Rock Hotel

Jl Kuta Beach, Kuta; tel: 0361-761869; www.hardrockhotels.net/bali; $$$

Hard Rock Hotel honours five decades of rock culture, its live music venues adorned with priceless rock 'n' roll memorabilia. There's an in-house radio station, a rock 'n' roll library, and a recording studio where rising stars can cut their own albums. The huge freeform pool has poolside cabins, together with the man-made 'Sand Island', where there's a night-time concert stage for accomplished bands.

Hotel Kumala Pantai

Jalan Werkudara, Legian Kaja, tel: 0361-755500; www.kumalapantai.com; $$

One of Bali's most popular hotels in this price range: regularly fully booked as it's great value for money, is well managed and has a pleasant beachside position. Has 88 rooms, a large 50-metre swimming pool and a beachside restaurant.

Padma Resort Bali at Legian

Jalan Padma 1, Legian; tel: 0361-752111; www.padmaresortbali.com; $$$

Rebranded from Hotel Padma Bali, the 404-room resort flaunts a whole host of new features and facilities, and some stunning contemporary sculptures. Facilities include the lovely new Padma Spa by Mandara, and a good choice of restaurants, such as the fine dining Bella Rosa Italian Restaurant.

Poppies Cottages I

Gang Poppies I, Kuta; tel: 0361-751059; www.poppies.net; $$

Romantic, traditional-style cottages set in private gardens with lily ponds and waterfalls. Each cottage has a thatched roof and a courtyard bathroom with open-air sunken bathtub. There are two swimming pools with landscaped sunbathing terraces, a garden restaurant, library and games area. It is often filled to capacity, so reservations are essential.

Un's Hotel

Jl Bene Sari 16, Kuta; tel: 0361-757409; www.unshotel.com; $

If you plan to stay in Kuta, you'll find that Un's Hotel is perfectly located, just five minutes' stroll from the beach on one side and five minutes' walk from the shops and nightspots of busy Jalan Legian on the other. For a budget hotel, this peaceful oasis is great value; its air-conditioned or fan-cooled rooms are bordered by wide communal balconies and terraces set around a swimming pool in a pretty garden.

Seminyak and Canggu

Dhyana Pura Beach Resort

Jalan Dhyana Pura; tel: 0361-730442; www.dhyanapura-beach-resort.com; $

Isolated, 113-room hotel with a friendly atmosphere and close to the beach. All rooms (some deluxe) have air-conditioning and hot water. Includes a pool and two restaurants.

Hotel Tugu Bali

Batu Bolong, Canggu; tel: 0361-731701;
www.tuguhotels.com; $$$$

A living museum of priceless antiques and rare cultural artefacts, this spellbinding boutique hotel and spa is set between rice fields and the quiet rugged beach of Canggu. The property is reminiscent of a village, with wooden houses overhanging cobbled alleyways bordered by hedges. Two suites contain replica studios of famous painters who discovered Bali in the 1930s. There is an exceptional spa, and the dining facilities include the atmospheric 300-year-old Kang Xi period temple.

The Legian

Jl Kayu Aya, Petitenget; tel: 0361-730622;
www.ghmhotels.com; $$$$

This all-suite hotel is set within lovely gardens beside a tranquil stretch of Seminyak Beach. Each spacious suite incorporates private balconies from which to take in the magnificent coastline view. The Legian's peaked roofs and bare wooden columns and rafters are the result of local craftsmanship, and intricate Indonesian sculptures greet you in the impressive lobby. There's a fabulous pool here and an excellent restaurant.

Mystique Apartments

Jalan Raya Petitenget 2000XX; tel: 0361-737415; www.balimystique.com; $$$

A small block of 16 luxury apartments set around a giant banyan tree amid pools. A five minute walk from the beach, most have two bedrooms and all have modern fittings. Facilities include a spa, swimming pool and restaurant.

The Oberoi

Jl Kayu Aya, Petitenget; tel: 0361-730361;
www.oberoihotels.com; $$$$

With a history that spans three decades, The Oberoi truly embraces the culture of the island. The hotel is positioned right beside the beach and comprises Balinese-style cottages and villas set in landscaped gardens. Other nice touches include villa pools, private courtyards and open-air massage parlours, while the main swimming pool is reminiscent of an ancient Balinese bathing place. There are two restaurants, recreational facilities and cultural performances.

Pelangi Bali Hotel

Jalan Dhyana Pura; tel: 0361-730346;
www.pelangibali.com; $$

Right on the beach front and close to the highly regarded Gado Gado restaurant. This small, two-storey hotel with 89 rooms has decently furnished rooms (plump for the larger deluxe room with living area if your budget stretches) and a swimming pool that overlooks the crashing surf of Seminyak beach.

Jimbaran Bay

Ayana Resort and Spa

Jl Karang Mas Sejahtera, Jimbaran;
tel: 0361-702222; www.ayanaresort.com;
$$$

Hotel Sanur Beach

This exceptional resort occupies a spectacular cliff-top setting. It offers a wide variety of accommodation as well as an almost overwhelming choice of recreational facilities, restaurants, spa venues, swimming pools, bars (including Rock Bar positioned on semi-offshore rocks) and wedding venues (including two avant-garde wedding chapels). The modern Balinese architecture is complemented by ornate doors, whimsical stone carvings and Indonesian artwork. Pools and waterfalls cascade towards the ocean, and a series of romantic open pavilions are encompassed by lotus ponds.

Four Seasons Resort

Jl Uluwatu, Jimbaran; tel: 0361-701010; www.fourseasons.com; $$$$

The gorgeous gardens of this luxury villa resort roll down to a beautiful sandy beach. The villas are spacious with thatched roofs, private gardens, plunge pools and secluded open-air bathrooms; the two sumptuous royal villas and nine private residences (with two, three and four bedrooms) have private swimming pools. Additionally, you'll find five restaurants, a multi-award-winning spa, and the Ganesha Art Gallery. Tennis courts and a cookery school are also on site.

The Bukit

The Beverly Hills

Jalan Goa Gong, Banjar Santhi Karya, Ungasan; tel: 0361-8481800; www.balibeverlyhills.com; $$$$

Glamorous, Korean-owned villa hotel located on a peaceful hill only 20 minutes' drive from the airport, with unbroken views extending across the bay and the Garuda Wisnu Kencana statue. Choose from one of the 25 one-, two- and three-bedroom villas, each with enormous en-suite bathrooms, walled gardens, private pools and relaxation *bales* (pavilions). Spa facilities and restaurant – romantic candlelit dinners on carpets of rose petals are a speciality.

Bulgari Resort

Jalan Goa Lempeh, Banjar Dinas Kangin, Uluwatu; tel: 0361-8471000; www.bulgari hotels.com; $$$$

Resting 160 metres/yds above the ocean at Bali's southernmost point, this designer resort is the second in a series to be built in prestigious locations around the world. The glamorous cliff-edge villa retreat and spa fuses chic Italian modernity with Indonesian artefacts and textiles. Overpriced villas, but the food served at the two restaurants is excellent. There are 56 one-bedroom and three two-bedroom villas, all with private plunge pools.

Karma Kandara

Banjar Wijaya Kusuma, Ungasan; tel: 0361-848 2200; www.karmakandara.com; $$$$

Blessed with an intoxicating view of the Indian Ocean, this stunning, five-star resort has everything that you could possibly require within a single package, including luxurious villa accom-

Balinese hotel style in Sanur

modation, 24-hour reception, security and room service, childcare amenities, a spectacular Balinese spa and a glamorous fine dining restaurant. It even has the facility of a private cliff inclinator, providing access to Karma Kandara's pristine beach, beach club and bar.

Rocky Bungalows

Off Jalan Uluwatu; tel: 081-7346209; $

This surfer hangout, three minutes' walk from the sea at Padang Padang, has ten pleasant balconied rooms and a relaxing atmosphere. Includes a simple restaurant.

Sanur

Bali Hyatt

Jl Bali Hyatt; tel: 0361-288271; www.bali hyatt.com; $$$

Bali Hyatt has been flourishing in Sanur for well over three decades, and its facilities are as complete as you will find anywhere in Bali. Accommodation consists of 390 rooms and suites, many with sea views; amenities include restaurants, swimming pools, a children's club, a convention centre and a gorgeous spa set within its own compound. However, it's the botanical gardens that add the real wow factor.

Hotel Sanur Beach

Jl Danau Tamblingan, Semawang; tel: 0361-288011; www.sanurbeachhotelbali.com; $$

This long-established hotel, with its four-storey block and exclusive bungalows set in landscaped gardens on the beach, is renowned for its friendly staff and excellent service. It offers a range of sports facilities and restaurants that serve Indonesian, Italian, Mexican and South American food.

La Taverna Hotel

Jalan Danau Tamblingan 29; tel: 0361-288497; www.latavernahotel.com; $$

Old hotel with a good reputation. Rooms are in the form of delightful thatched bungalows with Italian stucco walls, antique furniture and elegant décor. The hotel is set in a garden with a private beach, pool, bar and pizzeria. Includes 22 rooms, nine more expensive suites, and a good beachfront restaurant.

Tandjung Sari Hotel

Jalan Danau Tamblingan 41; tel: 0361-288441; www.tandjungsari.com; $$

A charming and historical hotel. Choose between a traditional Balinese-style bungalow or a villa with pavilion. All are set by the sea in lovely gardens with meandering paths. Has a swimming pool and restaurant but meals can be served privately in your own bungalow. This old-style, serene hotel is known for its excellent service and views.

Nusa Dua/Tanjung Benoa

Conrad Bali

Jl Pratama, Tanjung Benoa; tel: 0361-778788; www.conradhotels.com; $$$

Situated in a prime location on the long finger-shaped cape of Tanjung Benoa, this five-star resort attracts families,

Upmarket accommodation in Ubud

honeymooners and business travellers with a wide range of facilities and leisure options. A sparkling lagoon pool, complete with romantic Venetian-style bridges and a sandy-bottomed shallow area for kids, meanders past thatched massage pavilions, guest rooms, bars, restaurants and a 300m/yd crescent of pristine beach.

Grand Hyatt Bali

Nusa Dua; tel: 0361-771234/ 772038; www.hyatt.com; $$$

Grand Hyatt is the island's largest resort, served by five restaurants and numerous amenities. Styled after a fabled Balinese water palace, the hotel has an aquatic theme that begins at the lobby then ebbs and flows down to the ocean, transforming en route into lakes, moats, lagoons, rivers, waterfall-fed rock pools and swimming pools, linked by meandering pathways and straddled by hump-back bridges. The beautiful gardens are bordered by a 650m/yd white-sand beach offering sunbathing, safe swimming and water sports.

Nikko Bali Resort

Jalan Raya Nusa Dua, Selatan; tel: 0361-773377; www.nikkobali.com; $$$

Nikko Bali's dramatic clifftop setting is unique. Close to Nusa Dua but unencumbered by neighbours, the resort is built into the rock face with a private beach that would be inaccessible were it not for the lift that transports guests up and down the 15 storeys between the lush gardens and the rolling surf. Contains 390 rooms, five restaurants, three bars, an amphitheatre and a spa.

Ubud area

Four Seasons Sayan

Sayan, Ubud; tel: 0361-977577; www.fourseasons.com; $$$$

Sayan is just 10-15 minutes north of Ubud. This exclusive resort is situated on the banks of the Ayung River gorge. The approach is via a solid teak bridge, which leads to an awesome lotus pond, resting on the roof of the main building like a giant flying saucer hovering above the trees. The vista of the river as it coils its way through the chasm below is spectacular. Accommodation comprises 60 units; 42 of these are villas and the remaining 18 are suites. A treatment in the riverside spa is an experience that you will never forget.

Tegal Sari

Jl Hanoman, Padang Tegal, Ubud; tel: 0361-975376; www.tegalsari-ubud.com; $

This romantic hotel rests within an enviable, peaceful location in the middle of the rice fields, just 1.5km (1 mile) from the centre of Ubud. It offers the choice of rooms and duplex bungalows, each one different. There is also a swimming pool, a massage pavilion, an open-air fitness arena, dining *bales* (pavilions), lotus ponds and a restaurant. This is probably the best-value budget hotel in Ubud and extremely popular, so book well in advance.

Traditional-style architecture

Ubud Hanging Gardens

Desa Buahan, Desa Payangan; tel: 0361-982700; www.ubudhanginggardens.com; $$$$

Steeply set amid the rice terraces of Ubud are 38 private villas, each with its own infinity plunge pool and spa. The resort's Beduur restaurant, which serves wonderful French-Asian haute cuisine, is accessed by a private funicular. It clings to the side of a river gorge with views of a floodlit temple, which at night appears to be magically floating upon the clouds.

Ubud Village Hotel

Jalan Monkey Forest; tel: 0361-975571; www.ubudvillagehotel.com; $$

An elegant, medium-priced hotel that offers comfortable rooms and a selection of small luxury villas at the rear of the property, set close to a small river. Large swimming pool in pleasant surroundings, 23 rooms, five villas and a restaurant/bar.

Ulun Ubud

Sanggingan, Ubud; tel: 0361-975024; www.ulunubud.com; $$

A gem of a hotel carved into the hillside, this delightful place offers excellent value for money with spacious cottages, a restaurant and a spring-fed infinity pool presenting stunning views of the Campuhan River, the jungle and paddy fields. The hotel was created by a Balinese family of artists, so contains some beautiful artworks.

Kintamani/Batur

Lakeview Restaurant & Hotel

Penelokan, Kintamani; tel: 0366-51394; http://lakeviewbali.com/en/; $$

Perched on the rim of the ancient caldera, this place offers 20 spacious rooms, each with views of the volcano and lake from both the bed and the bathroom. You can watch the sunrise over the lake from your balcony, or sit out at night under the stars, enjoying the twinkling lights from the eight fishing villages known as *bintang danu* (stars of the lake) dotted around the water's edge.

Candidasa

Alila Manggis

Buitan, Manggis; tel: 0363-41011; www.alilahotels.com/Manggis; $$$$

This Green Globe-certified boutique resort in the peaceful beachside village of Manggis has won numerous awards for its commitment to responsible tourism. There's an organic garden, and the spa products are all-natural. The suites, rooms, restaurant, spa and swimming pool are set within a coconut grove garden that gently rolls on to Buitan Beach. The hotel is famous for its cookery school, which gives lessons in how to prepare Balinese cuisine.

Amankila Resort

Manggis, Karangasem; tel: 0363-41333; www.amankila.com; $$$$

The ultra-luxe Amankila Resort is comprised of a cluster of thatched pavilions,

Sweet–smelling room decoration

two restaurants, a private beach club and a spectacular three-tiered swimming pool, cascading downhill to shimmering Labuanamuk Bay – the vista is eye-boggling. The stand-alone suites rest on stilts, maximising the views; each features a shaded outdoor terrace, while nine enjoy private pools.

Amarta

Candidasa; tel: 0363-41230; $

If you're looking for budget accommodation, you can't go wrong with Amarta. These Western-owned beachside bungalows and stylish rooms are excellent value for money and a favourite with Bali's expats. The staff are friendly, there is a swimming pool, and the restaurant serves wholesome food and seriously good hearty breakfasts are included in the room rate. There is a choice of simple and rustic accommodation or new contemporary accommodation.

The Watergarden

Jalan Raya Candidasa; tel: 0363-41540; www.watergardenhotel. com; $$

The name of this delightful hotel says it all. The bungalows are scattered among lush gardens and ponds full of flora and fish. A favourite weekend retreat for many Bali residents. The English management is very hands-on, there are 12 rooms and the restaurant is excellent, with a variety of vegetarian dishes and some Thai options.

Nusa Lembongan
Hai Tide Huts

Mushroom Bay, Nusa Lembongan; tel: 0366-720331; www.balihaitidehuts.com; $$

Each of these romantic, rice-barn-style thatch and bamboo huts has a bedroom accessed by a ladder. Stylish and immaculate furnishings, combined with air conditioning and room service, transform this traditionally simple accommodation into something that is ethnically chic. The colourful bathrooms are shared and located a few metres from the huts. Facilities include a swimming pool, restaurant and beach club.

Lovina/Buleleng
Adirama

Jl Raya Lovina; tel: 0362-41759; www.adiramabeachhotel.com; $$

This old beach-front hotel is Dutch-owned and fairly recently renovated with attractive new furnishings and new bathrooms. Each room has a private balcony overlooking the swimming pool, and there is a small spa and attractive sea-front restaurant.

Bali Paradise Hotel

Jalan Kartika, Kalibukbuk; tel: 0362-41432; www.baliparadisehotel.com; $$

Fairly new hotel hidden in the rice fields halfway between the main road and the sea. Excellent value for money. The eight expansive rooms have great views and en-suite bathrooms with walk-in showers and bathtubs. There's a pleasant restaurant, bar and small spa.

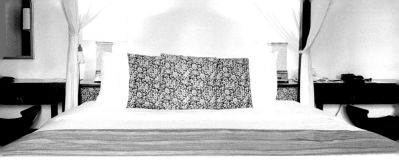

Boutique bedroom

Damai Lovina Villas

Jl Damai, Kayuputih, Lovina; tel: 0362-41008; www.damai.com; $$$$

Intimate retreat a short distance inland from Bali's north coast. It has just eight luxurious villa-style rooms, with four-poster beds, hand-carved doors and en suite bathrooms with jacuzzi tubs under the stars. The setting is a hidden paradise, with cascading gardens and an azure sea shimmering in the distance. The resort harvests its own rice and organic produce, which is then served in its renowned gourmet restaurant.

Bedugul

Pacung Mountain Resort

Jl Raya Pacung, Baturiti; tel: 0368-21038/9; www.pacungbali.com; $$

This hillside resort is the only hotel in the area with a swimming pool; it also has a beautiful vista of the valley and Gunung (Mt) Batukau. Accommodation is comprised of rooms, or attractive thatched cottages with balconies and rice-field views. A gondola transports guests from their rooms to the pool. There is also a restaurant, but no air conditioning in this cool climate.

Tabanan

Cempaka Belimbing Villas

Belimbing; tel: 0361-7451178; www.cempakabelimbing.com; $$

Northwest of Tabanan town in the foot-hills of Gunung Batukau is the pretty village of Belimbing, located south of Sanda. The 14 bungalows are set in rice fields; some have views of the rice terraces while others face the valley or the gardens and pool. It's a delight to sit on the verandah and just chill. Has a restaurant, large swimming pool and a tour desk that organises excursions in the local area.

Gajah Mina Beach Resort

Suraberata, Lalanglinggah, Selemadeg, Tabanan; mobile: 081-934-355633; www.gajahminaresort.com; $$

This charming hotel offers individual Balinese-style villas, a restaurant and a swimming pool, all spread across a dazzling headland surmounting a private beach. The restaurant is a delight, utilising fresh produce from the hotel's own garden. It is remote, but an ideal choice for those looking to escape the hustle and bustle of the tourist areas.

Taro

Elephant Safari Park Lodge

Jalan Elephant Park, Taro, Tegallalang; tel: 0361-721480; www.elephantsafaripark lodge.com; $$$$

Pack a trunk and stay over for a night or two in the luxurious safari-style lodge of the Elephant Safari Park. It offers a swimming pool, bar, lounge, gym, spa and four different styles of air-conditioned accommodation, with big windows and terraces for elephant watching. Elegant interiors are set off by custom-made, elephant-themed accessories, such as bed legs crafted in the form of elephant feet.

Gianyar food market

RESTAURANTS

New restaurants open and close all the time in Bali. The following selection includes tried-and-tested establishments, plus new finds; this is just the tip of the iceberg, of course. Many hotels also have restaurants serving good food. In the tourist centres of Sanur, Kuta/Legian and Nusa Dua, restaurants usually serve lunch from 11am–3pm, and dinner (some with dance performances) from 6–10pm daily. A number of restaurants open all day, including for breakfast. In Ubud, Lovina and Candidasa, restaurants open from 11am–9pm daily, unless they serve breakfast.

Sanur was the first area to attract Western tourists and is still Bali's largest expatriate area today. The variety is expanding rapidly and new restaurants open regularly. Denpasar sees mostly locals and domestic tourists, hence the many small Indonesian and Chinese restaurants in the capital city, particularly along Jalan Teuku Umar. Don't expect much in terms of Western fare.

In Kuta, the surfer haven, originally the only food choices here were cheap eats in the two lanes near the Poppies Hotel and uninspiring food served at hotels on the beach front and along Jalan Legian. These days, the professionals are moving in and the quality (and prices) fast rising, but the backpacker cheapies still exist along the many lanes that wind around Kuta. For inexpensive and delicious grilled seafood at night, head for the Kuta Night Market. The food is very easy on the pocket just as long as you avoid going for the lobster.

Tuban, sometimes referred to as South Kuta, has suddenly come to life with the opening of a slew of good restaurants. Legian is a favourite area for families and most of the local restaurants reflect this. Expect basic simple food and invariably good value.

In Seminyak you'll find a mix of late-night bars and excellent restaurants. The so-called 'Eat Street' – the loop from Jalan Laksmana/Kayu Aya through Jalan Petitenget – offers a huge range of cuisines at great prices. Seminyak has the highest concentration of independent fine-dining restaurants on the island.

In Jimbaran Bay, although the choices are fairly slim outside of the hotels, try the grilled seafood places that open around sunset along the beach. Expect lots of smoke from the open-air barbecues but a pleasant setting and food that is usually good. The restaurant

> Price for a two-course meal for one including a non-alcoholic beverage:
> $$$$ = over Rp 300,000
> $$$ = Rp 200,000–300,000
> $$ = Rp 100,000–200,000
> $ = below Rp 100,000

Fish drying at Kendongan fish market, near Jimbaran

pickings are slim in the Nusa Dua/Tanjung Benoa area and mainly confined to the large luxury hotels.

In the Batur and Kintamani area, lunch buffets – strictly Indonesian fare – are served in the many restaurants along the ridge at Penelokan. For evening meals, go to the small hotels or the simple *warung* down by the lake at Toya Bungkah.

Most restaurants in Candidasa serve grilled seafood along with other standard Indonesian dishes. Like Ubud, this is another area that is beginning to see foreign professionals opening more international-style restaurants.

Sanur

Café Batujimbar
Jl Danau Tamblingan 75, Sanur; tel: 0361-287374; $$

This is a popular street-side café and long-time favourite of people who know Sanur. Dining takes place in an open-sided pavilion or alfresco under the trees. Italian and Mexican dishes grace the menu, including pastas and quesadillas, together with healthy salads, home-made breads and cakes, herbal teas and booster fruit juices. Organic vegetables and herbs are grown at the owner's farm near Bedugul.

Massimo il Ristorante
Jl Danau Tamblingan 206, Sanur; tel: 0361-288942; $$

This is a great Italian restaurant, set in an attractive open pavilion surrounded by a garden. The menu offers authentic specialities from Lecce in southeast Italy, where the owner-chef Massimo hails from. The pasta dishes and thin-crust wood-fired oven pizzas are all good. Massimo also does an excellent risotto with mushrooms and Italian sausage, as well as beef fillets, chicken, duck and fish specialities, and the best Italian ice cream in Bali.

Mezzanine Restaurant & Bar
Jl Danau Tamblingan 63, Sanur; tel: 0361-270624; $$$

A stylish restaurant with helpful and friendly staff and an interesting blend of Thai, Japanese, Chinese and Western dishes on the menu. The colonial-style building, vast, open-sided and broad-pillared, features a varied choice of dining areas – from breezy terrace at the front to cosy mezzanine. The menu choice includes a *teppanyaki* grill and seafood from the large fish tank.

Sanur Beach Market
Jl Segara Ayu on the beach; tel: 0361-289374; $

This beach-side restaurant is excellent for grilled seafood and dessert. Choose the dance performance and special set dinner on one day a week, or order from the menu without cover charge.

Stiff Chilli
Jl Kesumasari 11, Semawang; tel: 0361-288371; $$

Dining in Seminyak

A rustic open-sided pavilion beside the beach, serving Italian cuisine with an Asian twist. This highly respected restaurant is famous for its crispy-skinned, grilled sausages, freshly baked ciabatta bread, authentic Italian pizzas and pasta delights, such as the tri-coloured fettuccine topped with creamy smoked marlin sauce.

Denpasar

Danau Toba

Jl Teuku Umar 74X; tel: 0361-263553; $$

Danau Toba is named after a famous lake in Sumatra, and the Chinese-Indonesian food served here comes from Medan in the same area. The menu offers a choice of small, medium, or large portions of fish, lobster, crab, prawn, squid, pigeon, duck, chicken, tofu, beef, frog and vegetables in a wide selection of different sauces. The rather gaudy Chinese decor features lucky mobiles and kitsch artwork, spinning circular tables facilitate the sharing of dishes, and tanks of live fish promise some incredibly fresh dishes.

Rasa Sayang

Jl Teuku Umar, Denpasar; tel: 0361-262006; $$

Local people claim that this Chinese restaurant is one of the best in Denpasar. The interior is simple, the decor is plain, and although the supermarket-style piped music doesn't do much for the ambience, the delicious food compensates for the lack of atmosphere. Delicacies include fish-head soup, lettuce buns, raw lobster with wasabi, deep-fried squid in Worcester sauce and sliced beef with Chinese broccoli.

Kuta/Legian

ExtraBlatt

Jalan Nakula 17, Legian; tel: 0361-732982; $

Small *warung* serving good simple German food, such as meatloaf and several types of *wurst* (sausage). Open daily.

Kori Restaurant & Bar

Jl Gang Poppies II, Kuta; tel: 0361-758605; $$$

Escape from the Kuta crowds to this quiet retreat with wonderful Balinese ambience and a lotus pond nearby; pick from low-cushioned seating or colonial-style chairs and marble-topped tables. The international menu offers delicious fresh seafood, imported steaks, favourites such as chargrilled bangers and mash, and warm sticky-toffee date pudding topped with butterscotch sauce.

Kunyit Bali

Hotel Santika, Jalan Kartika, Tuban (south Kuta); tel: 0361-751267; $

Any one of its special menus offers a taste of indigenous Bali. Specials include green papaya and snail soup, pork stewed in turmeric and sweet soy, and *ayam panggang kalasan* – chicken cooked in spiced coconut milk.

Grilling satay by the roadside, Denpasar

Ma Joly
Kupu Kupu Barong Beach Resort, Tuban (south Kuta); tel: 0361-753780; $$$$
Chic beachside French restaurant – sit indoors or on the beach. Try the *fricassee* of garoupa with prawns or toro tuna black pepper steak. Daily lunch specials are a bargain.

Made's Warung
Jl Pantai Kuta; tel: 0361-755297; $$
One of the first places to cater for foreigners when it was one of only two eateries on Kuta's main street, and still popular for its menu of local and international dishes and delicious desserts. A second branch, Made's Warung II (tel: 0361-732130) is located in Seminyak.

Poppies Restaurant
Gang Poppies I, Kuta; tel: 0361-751059; $$$
Poppies Restaurant has been serving punters since 1973 and enjoys a romantic garden setting, amid pools and fountains sheltered by pergolas draped in cascading thunbergia. Open for breakfast, lunch and dinner, with free WiFi from 8am until 7pm, Poppies offers a good selection of Asian and Western dishes including fresh fish and seafood, home-made soups, salads, pasta dishes and steaks. There are plenty of classic Indonesian specialities, while vegetarians are also well catered for.

Rosso Vivo
Jl Pantai Kuta, tel: 0361-751961; $$
With a casual atmosphere, live music, a choice of alfresco dining beside a swimming pool or on comfortable lounge seating within the stylish interior, and a wonderful menu of authentic Italian cuisine, it is no wonder that this restaurant is so popular.

TJ's Mexican Restaurant
Gang Poppies I; tel: 0361-751093; $$
This popular restaurant is known for its colourful decor and garden setting. The menu offers superb, authentic Californian-Mexican cuisine with delicious starters and the best loaded nachos, buffalo wings, quesadillas, tacos, enchiladas, tostadas, fajitas and margaritas this side of the Pacific. Try the aubergine or tofu and bean dip with chips and finish with the mango cheesecake with raspberry sauce.

Seminyak

Gateway of India
Jl Abimanyu, Seminyak; tel: 0361-732940; $$
With an Indian owner married to a Balinese, you can be assured of authentic Indian fare. The tandoori dishes and the freshly baked naan breads are wonderful, and be sure to try the lamb or chicken *kathi* roll, a sort of pancake bursting with a spicy filling. Very casual, so dress down for dinner. There are also branches in Sanur (tel: 0361-281579) and Kuta (tel: 0361-754463).

The Junction
Jl Laksmana/Kayu Aya, Seminyak;

Preparing lawar (meat, veg, coconut and spices) for a festival

tel: 0361-735610; $$
The Junction features funky architecture and interior design, with a variety of seating areas, including a lounge. It specialises in organic salads made with gourmet ingredients and also does sassy sandwiches in the form of panini, pitta pockets, crêpes and baguettes.

Ku De Ta
Jl Laksmana, Petitenget; tel: 0361–736969; $$$$
Bali's famous restaurant, beach club and sophisticated hotspot is the place to see and be seen, especially at sunset, when the setting is spectacular. Ku De Ta offers hearty breakfasts, excellent lunches and intimate dining at night, with a classy menu of contemporary Australian cuisine.

La Lucciola Restaurant & Bar
Jl Kayu Aya, Petitenget; tel: 0361-261047; $$$
Delicious Mediterranean and Italian food and a casual atmosphere are the hallmarks of this big, two-level thatched structure, which looks out over the beach. It's great for sunset cocktails and is usually packed for dinner. Reservations are essential, otherwise expect to wait at least an hour for a table.

Mama San
Jl Raya Kerobokan 135, Seminyak; tel: 0361-730436; $$$$
Mama San serves pungent Asian comfort food in fine-dining style within a purpose-designed industrial warehouse with a Shanghai Grand-era vibe. Enjoy a pre-dinner cocktail on tan leather chesterfields in the upstairs lounge, reminiscent of a bourgeois gentlemen's club, then dine downstairs on Chinese, Indonesian, Indian, Malay, Singaporean, Thai, Cambodian and Vietnamese cuisine.

Métis
Jl Petitenget 6; tel: 0361-737888; $$$$
This large and sophisticated fine dining restaurant, bar, lounge and gallery overlooks a rice field and a huge lotus pond. It serves French-Mediterranean cuisine and the menu includes the famous pan-seared hot foie gras with port and raspberry reduction, morelo cherry and roasted apple.

Mykonos Taverna
Jl Laksmana 57; tel: 0361-733253; $$
A small, simple, traditional Greek tavern with *bouzouki* music to match. Wonderful Greek dips, plus fish and lamb dishes at reasonable prices, can be ordered. Open for lunch and dinner.

La Sal
Jl Drupadi 100; tel: 0361-738321; $$$
Expect an excellent selection of inventive tapas and main courses at this Spanish eaterie. An Argentinian-style *churrasco* meal of grilled meats is served nightly.

Wood-fired pizza oven in a Seminyak restaurant

Sardine

Jl Petitenget; tel: 0361-738202; $$$$

The extraordinary Sardine features a polished bamboo bar and a gourmet menu, where the emphasis is on fresh fish and seafood – meat and vegetarian dishes do get a look in too. The restaurant overlooks a working rice field, which the owners have purchased in order to protect their views and then embellished with special lighting, coloured flags and giant urns.

Sarong

Jl Petitenget No. 19X; tel: 0361-4737809; www.sarongbali.com; $$$$

The sumptuous quirkiness of Sarong makes it feel so cosy that you could be mistaken for thinking you've walked into someone's home. The menu features the great cuisines of Southeast Asia, with a twist. Open daily from 6.30pm until midnight, this is one of Bali's best and most popular fine-dining restaurants. Reservations are essential.

Sate Bali

Jl Laksmana; tel: 0361-736734; $$

For a superlative introduction to Balinese food, order the multi-course *rijsttafel* dinner. Sate Bali also runs an excellent cooking class – the owner and chef has a background in leading five-star hotels.

Taco Beach

Jl Kunti, Seminyak; $

Small and simple restaurant beside the street with a cheerful colourful décor serving superb Californian-Mexican food, including Balinese fusion dishes such as the *babi guling* burritos and *babi guling* tacos. Ingredients are fresh and prices are ridiculously low.

Trattoria

Jl Laksmana/Kayu Aya; tel: 0361-737082; $$

Packed almost every night of the week, which says a lot about the food (and the reasonable prices) here. There are fantastic pastas, pizzas and salads as well as beef and seafood dishes, but be prepared to wait if you don't have a reservation. Tables are packed tightly together in this smallish restaurant with a lively atmosphere.

Jimbaran Bay

A particularly good seafood place on the beach is **Ayu Wandira** (tel: 0361-701950; $$), which dishes up a huge barbecued seafood platter.

Sundara

Four Seasons Resort, Jimbaran Bay; tel: 0361-708333; www.sundarabali.com; $$$$

Beach club by day and sophisticated restaurant by night, Sundara at Four Seasons Jimbaran comprises a variety of indoor and outdoor spaces with fabulous ocean views. Here, an alfresco patio sits between two Balinese-style pavilions, one of which covers two levels complete with an open kitchen and

Oysters and sushi at Ku De Ta

bar. Elevated above the sandy shore is a spectacular infinity lap pool. Open daily from 11am until 1am, the lunch menu offers wood-fired pizza, sushi and Balinese delights, while the dinner menu presents gourmet steak and seafood selections.

Nusa Dua/Tanjung Benoa

Bumbu Bali

Jl Pratama, Tanjung Benoa; tel: 0361-774502; $$$

'Bumbu' means spice paste, and this restaurant is renowned for its long menu of authentic, beautifully presented Balinese dishes – seafood and duck in banana leaf lead the specialities. You can also sign up for cookery classes, and free transport to Bumbu Bali is provided by hotels in the area. Traditional Balinese dance shows are held some nights.

Nampu

Grand Hyatt, Nusa Dua; tel: 0361-771234; $$$$

A superb Japanese fine-dining restaurant with a choice of eating experiences including a *teppanyaki* room, private *tatami* rooms and a sophisticated dining room. Serves beautifully presented, high-quality sashimi, sushi, tempura, charcoal-grilled dishes and much more.

The Italian Restaurant

Amanusa, Nusa Dua; tel: 0361-772333; $$$$

Rather unimaginative name but all is forgiven when you try its well-executed elegant Italian dishes either in air-conditioned comfort or on the romantic garden terrace.

Ubud

Barberkyu Kafe

Jalan Monkey Forest; tel: 0361-976177; $$

Serves a mix of international and Indonesian food with an emphasis on barbecued meats. Many types of sausages (chorizo, bratwurst and the Balinese *urutan*) plus ribs, steaks, kebabs and prawns.

Bebek Bengil (Dirty Duck)

Jl Hanuman, Padangtegal; tel: 0361-975489; $$

An Ubud institution, this sprawling open-air garden restaurant and bar is surrounded by rice fields with numerous cosy and intimate spots for eating and drinking. It promotes popular local dishes and European-style home cooking, with an extensive menu that includes Bali's famous crispy duck, as well as bratwurst and mash, *nasi campur*, imported steaks and old-fashioned apple crumble.

Café des Artistes

Jalan Bisma 9X; tel: 0361-972706; www.cafedesartistesbali.com; $$

This is one of Ubud's best-value restaurants and has a pleasant garden setting. Open daily, reservations are

Coffee and spices

Bebek betutu (steamed duck) and accompaniments

essential most evenings. It offers Belgian specialities such as *carbonades à la flamande* (beef stewed in black beer) and steaks, as well as some Indonesian and Thai dishes thrown in for good measure. A Belgian beer makes the perfect accompaniment to your meal.

Casa Luna

Jl Raya Ubud; tel: 0361-973283; $$

This semi open-air, café-style restaurant on different levels has a laid-back vibe and is renowned for its Sunday brunch, breakfast and cakes. The menu options are international and Indonesian specialities, and include vegetarian spring rolls, smoked marlin salad, spiced coconut fish and delectable offerings from the Honeymoon Bakery.

Ibu Oka

Jl Suweta; tel: 0361-976345; $

The most famous outlet in Bali for *babi guling*, the island's most revered dish – from opening (11am) until around 2.30pm there is a constant queue. When the street is closed for royal ceremonies, the *warung* operates from the owner's house at Jalan Tegal Sari 2 nearby.

Lamak

Monkey Forest Road, Ubud; tel: 0361-974668; www.lamakbali.com; $$$$

This fine-dining restaurant is decorated in a funky, flamboyant take on the traditional. The menu is a marriage of Asian food with recipes from the south of France, the Mediterranean and Asia, such as coconut-crusted, pan-fried chicken breast filled with mango on yellow turmeric sauce. Open daily 10am–11pm, you can dine alfresco or in an air-conditioned area inside.

Mozaic

Jl Raya Sanggingan; tel: 0361-975768; www.mozaic-bali.com; $$$$

Mozaic is the only restaurant in Indonesia to have received the accolade of entry in the worldwide guide *Les Grandes Tables du Monde*. Tables spill out into a romantic candlelit garden, and the eclectic cuisine, with its French-style presentation, attracts discerning gourmets. Chef-owner Chris Salans believes that fixed menus are restrictive, so his ever-changing list of creations is reprinted on a daily basis, as dishes evolve, disappear and return in accordance with market availability. The best way to sample the cuisine is through the seven-course tasting menu that may include delights such as rosemary-braised ocean trout fillet and spiced organic pumpkin purée, in a roasted-onion Spanish saffron emulsion. Closed on Monday.

Tut Mak

Jl Dewi Sita; tel: 0361-975754; $$

This friendly café-style restaurant offers a variety of eating areas and is popular with expats. It serves great breakfasts, and its omelettes are a highlight, but sandwiches, burgers, dips, snacks and

Bringing offerings to a temple festival

full meals, including Indonesian specialities, all put in an appearance too. There is also a children's menu.

Batur and Kintamani

Lakeview Hotel

Penelokan; tel: 0366-51394; $$

The Lakeview Hotel restaurant is perched on a mountain ridge with awesome views from picture windows and a narrow terrace that offers alfresco dining. Open daily from 8am–10pm, it serves a daily buffet breakfast including delicious banana fritters, followed by a traditional Indonesian buffet (from 11am daily).

Nyoman Mawa 'Under the Volcano'

Jl Batur Tengah, Toya Bungkah; tel: 0366-51166; $

This restaurant is linked to a small hotel, and situated lakeside in an open-sided pavilion with the volcano towering above. Serves simple international dishes and local fare including the house speciality of sweet fish from the lake. Open daily 7am–9pm.

Bedulu, Tampaksiring and Tegallalang

Elephant Park Restaurant

Jl Elephant Park Taro, Tegallalang; tel: 0361-721480; $$$

The restaurant inside the park overlooks the lake where the elephants bathe. Serves a buffet daily between 11am and 3pm, with good-quality Western and Asian cuisine. Dinner is for Safari Park Lodge guests only.

Klungkung and Besakih

Lihat Sawah

Banjar Tebola, Sidemen, Karangasem; tel: 0366-530 0516/ 530 0519; www. lihatsawah.com; $$

This charming restaurant in the rice fields is part of a small and friendly, family-run guesthouse. Semi open-air, it offers spectacular views of the countryside. The menu includes simple European, Thai and Indonesian specialities. Open daily 7am–10pm.

Candidasa

Candi Agung

Jalan Raya Candidasa; tel: 0363-41672; $

Small clean *warung* that features a Balinese dance performance every evening at 8pm, when one of the waitresses changes into costume and performs on a small stage at the front. Simple, well-executed Indonesian Chinese dishes, many featuring chicken and fish. Especially good is *udung goring*, or grilled prawns with Balinese *sambal*.

Garpu

Jl Raya Sengkidu, Candidasa; tel: 0363-49174; $$

This quality restaurant is situated right beside the sea, with a lounge and a poolside area. Garpu means 'fork' in Indonesian, and this theme is reflected in the stylish architecture and interior design. The *à la carte, table d'hôte*

Nasi goreng (fried rice)　　　　*A food cart plies its wares, Gianyar*

and buffet menus showcase specialities from the Mediterranean (especially France and Italy) and Bali.

Lovina/Buleleng

Adirama
Adirama Beach Hotel, Lovina; tel: 0362-41759; $$

Hotel restaurant right at the water's edge serving everything from fish and chips to Indonesian butter fried chicken. Also features a good selection of Mexican dishes, such as tacos, enchiladas, quesadillas and crunchy taquitos.

Jasmine Kitchen
Gang Bina Ria, off Jalan Bina Ria, Kalibukbuk, Lovina; tel: 0362-41565; $$

Small Thai eatery whose vegetarian spring rolls, served with sweet chilli sauce, are perfect. Also recommended is their *massamam* curry with coconut milk, potatoes and peanuts, either with prawns or vegetables.

Khi Khi Seafood Restaurant
Kalibukbuk, Lovina; tel: 0362-41548; $

An old favourite, this long-established, large seafood restaurant is very popular with the locals. Serves Indonesian and Japanese cuisine ranging from sushi, *mie goring* and *nasi goring* to grilled fresh fish, prawns and calamari. A variety of Chinese specialities, such as *cap cay* and sweet and sour dishes, are also available.

Warung Aria
Jalan Raya Lovina 18, Kalibukbuk, Lovina; tel: 0362-41341; $

Perennially busy small *warung* on main road serving simple (and cheap) Cantonese-style dishes such as a superlative fried rice studded with shrimps.

Krambitan, Pupuan and Medewi

Naga Restaurant
Gajah Mina Beach Resort, Suraberata, Lalanglinggah, Selemadeg, Tabanan; tel: 081-934-355633; www.gajahminaresort.com; $$–$$$

Gentle sea breezes waft across the terrace of Naga's partly open pavilion. The chef Bagus prepares fresh seafood dishes, pizzas, pasta, classic French and Thai creations and local delicacies such as banana flower curry using produce grown in his own fruit, vegetable and herb garden. Open daily 8am–10.30pm.

Plantations
Sanda Butik Villas, Desa Sanda, Pupuan; tel: 0828-372 0055; www.sandavillas.com; $$

This open-air restaurant is set within the coffee-plantation grounds of a small hotel, offering glorious views over rice fields and a wooded valley. Open daily 7am–9pm, its extensive menu includes pasta, stir-fries, curries, Indonesian dishes and great salads using locally grown lettuces, asparagus, herbs and mushrooms. Also serves locally harvested coffee.

Live music performance

NIGHTLIFE

There is no shortage of nightclubs, dance-bars, discos and live music venues in Bali's tourist areas. Kuta tends to get going earlier than Seminyak and closes earlier, at around 3 or 4am. The dance-bars in Seminyak usually start getting busy at around 11pm; at some of these, you can party until sunrise, but don't expect them to start pumping until about 2am.

The bars in Sanur generally close at midnight. Here, the scene is more relaxed and mellow, with a few low-key dance clubs that attract a more mature crowd. Older Indonesian businessmen often frequent them, more as a place to relax than for the dancing.

There's not much nightlife in Ubud, and the majority of venues here close before midnight. Nusa Dua is not an area known for its nightlife scene, although every hotel has its own bars and sometimes a nightclub. Gambling is illegal in Indonesia, so there are no casinos.

Below are listed the most popular venues, some of them full-service restaurants with bars and live music.

Kuta/Legian

Centerstage
Hard Rock Hotel, Jl Pantai, Kuta; tel: 0361-5761869
A refined and hi-tech venue dominated by an enormous 5m (16ft) video screen and a plethora of rock memorabilia.

Presents live music and entertainment every night from 8.30pm until 11.30pm. Slick local bands sing popular covers from a raised stage positioned inside and above the circular central bar, surrounded by video screens and sophisticated lighting. Centerstage doesn't impose a cover charge, but expect to pay upmarket hotel prices for your drinks.

M-Bar-Go
Jl Legian; tel: 0361-756280
M-Bar-Go is a gargantuan nightclub covering two floors with an urban-chic industrial theme, minimal lighting, dark decor and an underground vibe. Glass doors at the front open into a vast, air-conditioned interior space, where resident and guest DJs play booming house music attracting a mixed crowd of surfers, tourists and locals.

Sky Garden
Jl Legian, Kuta; tel: 0361-755423
One of the most pumping venues in Kuta and a veritable hot spot for a sophisticated cocktail to start your evening around town. This multi-levelled restaurant and open-air rooftop lounge, where you can listen to music and chill on comfy sofas, towers above the street.

Seminyak

Ku De Ta
Jalan Laksmana, Seminyak; tel: 0361-

Alfresco drinking in Jimbaran

736969; www.kudeta.net

Bali's most famous, sleek and trendy fine-dining restaurant, bar and nightlife venue. Hosts dance parties, fashion shows and internationally renowned DJs. Wide choice of seating indoors and by the beach. Attracts a sophisticated crowd.

Mannekepis

Jl Raya Seminyak; tel: 0361-8475784

A jazz and blues venue and Belgian bistro rolled into one, Mannekepis has a beautifully styled interior with a long bar. Live jazz, blues and rock are performed here on Wednesday, Thursday, Friday and Saturday nights. Upstairs is another large dining area, which spills onto an open-air terrace, complemented by a pool table and table football.

Maria Magdalena

Jl Abimanyu (Dhyana Pura) 6, Seminyak; tel: 0361-731622

Alfresco terrace bar and dance club on two levels with pool tables. Great entertainment provided with a midnight show and excellent DJ music. A very popular venue on Friday and Saturday nights, it doesn't get busy until after 11pm.

Mint

Jl Raya Petitenget 919 Seminyak, tel: 0361-4732 884

A chic dance club serving food and cocktails, it features a club lounge, a 25-metre central bar, and a booth with a bar-stage structure from which DJs play electronic house and pop while punters dance late into the night.

Mixwell

Jl Abimanyu (Dhyana Pura) No. 6, Seminyak; tel: 0361-736864

This popular gay venue is a small lounge bar with an outside terrace. It features DJ music, comedy drag shows and lip-synching divas.

Sanur

Arena Sports Bar

Jl ByPass I Gusti Ngurah Rai 115, Sanur; tel: 0361-287255

A lively pub-style venue, popular with Bali's expats and a fun place to catch a soccer match or a game of Aussie Rules on the big screen. Trivia quiz on Wednesday nights, and live music and pool competition on Friday nights.

Jazz Bar and Grille

Komplek Sanur Raya, J. Bypass Ngurah Rai; tel: 0361-285892

Regular live entertainment performed by well-respected jazz bands from Bali and beyond. The atmosphere is comfortable and cultured, and there is capacity for about 140 people over the two levels.

Ubud

Ozigo

Jl Sanggingan; tel: 0361-081 2367 9736

Ubud's only nightclub, offering live music at weekends, a dance floor, open-air terrace, and an intimate VIP lounge. Free transport service offered within the Ubud area.

Preparing for a temple festival

A–Z

A

Addresses

Street names can be a cause of confusion in Bali, because many have been renamed due to historical or political figures falling in and out of fashion. In many cases a street is still referred to by its old name, but the signpost will show the new version. Additionally, in tourist areas it is not uncommon for a street to have a western 'nickname' (eg Double Six Street), taken from a long-established restaurant or club that perhaps dominates the street. Note that 'Jl' stands for *Jalan*, which means 'Street'.

Age restrictions

In Bali and Indonesia the age of consent for heterosexual sexual activity is 19 years for males and 16 years for females. The age of consent for homosexuals is 18. The legal age for drinking is 18.

B

Budgeting

Some average costs: a beer Rp 25,000; glass of house wine Rp 45,000 (local) or Rp 100,000–120,000 (imported); a main course at a local *warung* (café) Rp 20,000–30,000, moderate restaurant Rp 80,000, expensive restaurant Rp 150,000–250,000; a cheap hotel US$25–60, moderate hotel US$60–200, deluxe hotel US$200–1,000. Taxi journey to/from the main airport Rp 35,000–335,000; single bus ticket Rp 100,000.

C

Children

Children are universally loved in Bali. Babysitters are available at major hotels, and many hotels and resorts offer children's activities, crèche facilities and children's clubs. Some of these facilities are free of charge to hotel guests, while other hotels charge a daily or hourly rate – ask when booking.

Clothing

Bring casual clothing of lightweight natural fabrics, such as cotton or linen, which offer the best comfort in the heat and humidity. Bali has a thriving garment industry, and clothes are readily available. Sandals or footwear that can be slipped off easily are a good idea, especially if planning to visit people's homes – shoes are always removed before going into a house. You'll need a light jacket or sweater if you're planning to visit mountain spots, and for air-conditioned buildings or vehicles.

Religious ceremony held when building a new home

Crime and safety

While personal safety is not a general problem in Bali, as with anywhere in the world it is important to be vigilant with your belongings. Pickpockets, car break-ins and drive-by bag snatching seem to be the most common complaints. It is not recommended to walk alone along Kuta beach at night. To reduce your risk, take the same basic precautions you would if you were visiting a big city.

All thefts should be reported immediately to the police, even though there is little chance of recovering stolen belongings. This applies especially to passports and other official documents. Without a police report, you will have difficulty obtaining new documents and leaving the country, or claiming on your insurance policy.

All narcotics are illegal in Indonesia. The use, sale or purchase of narcotics results in very long prison terms – even death – and/or huge fines. Don't keep or carry packages for strangers.

Customs

In addition to your embarkation card, a customs declaration form must be completed before arrival.

Indonesian regulations strictly prohibit the entry of weapons, narcotics and pornography. Fresh fruits, plants, animal products and exposed films and videos should be declared and may be checked or even confiscated. Photographic equipment, laptop computers and other electronics can be brought in provided that they are taken out on departure. A maximum of 1 litre of alcohol, 200 cigarettes or 50 cigars or 100 grams of tobacco, and a reasonable amount of perfume may be brought in. There is no restriction either on the import or the export of foreign currencies and traveller's cheques. However, the import and export of Indonesian currency exceeding Rp 10 million is prohibited.

The export of antiques more than 50 years old is not permitted; neither can ivory, tortoiseshell or crocodile skin be taken out.

Disabled Travellers

The Balinese believe that all physical and mental disabilities are punishments for improper behaviour in past lives. That said, people with physical disabilities are viewed with compassion. Generally, there is very little consciousness in Indonesia about the special needs of disabled people. Due to rough and broken pavements, high kerbs, open storm drains, an abundance of steps and a lack of ramps, it is difficult to move around Bali in a wheelchair. However, you will never have problems finding people who are willing to help you. Make sure your wheelchair is in good working order before you come to Bali, as you may find it hard to locate a repair shop.

E

Electricity

Indonesia (including Bali) uses the 220-volt system, 50 cycles and a round, two-pronged slim plug; adapters are readily available. Power failures are common, with a number of all-day scheduled power cuts, but most hotels and restaurants have back-up generators. Bathroom shaver plugs usually have a transformer switch.

Embassies and consulates

Australia and Canada
Jl Hayam Wuruk 88 B, Tanjung Bungkak, Denpasar; tel: 0361-241118; www.dfat.gov.au/bali.
Consular hours: Mon–Fri 8am–noon and 12.30–4pm.
Visa hours: Mon–Fri 8.30am–noon.

UK and Ireland
Jl Tirta Nadi 20, Sanur, Denpasar; tel: 0361-270601; email: bcbali@dps.centrin.net.id.
Opening hours: Mon–Fri 8.30am–12.30pm.

US
Jl Hayam Wuruk No. 188, Denpasar; tel: 0361-233605; email: amcobali@indosat.net.id.
Opening hours: Mon–Fri 8am–noon and 1–4.30pm.
Consulates for Czech Republic, Finland, Germany, Japan, Norway and Spain are also in Bali, but some are in Jimbaran or Sanur rather than Denpasar.

Emergencies

Bali has an Emergency Response Centre, so you just need to dial **112** to be put through to the communication centre that co-ordinates all of its emergency services. You can also call:
Ambulance **118**
Fire Department **113**
Police **110**
Search & Rescue **111/115/151**

Etiquette

The Balinese are remarkably friendly and courteous, even with so many visitors to their tiny island. They are also conservative, for tradition is the backbone of their culture.

Shaking hands on introduction is usual nowadays for both men and women. However, using the left hand to give or to receive something is taboo (the left hand is for personal hygiene purposes and therefore considered unclean), as is pointing with the left hand. Never touch anyone, even a child, on the head; a person's head is considered to be the most sacred part of the body. Crooking a finger to call someone is impolite; instead, beckon to the person by waving the fingers together with the palm facing down. Anger is not openly displayed, therefore aggressive gestures and postures, such as standing with your hands on your hips when talking, are considered

Celebrating Nyepi (Balinese New Year)

to be insulting. Avoid pointing with the index finger as this gesture may be taken as a physical challenge.

It is also offensive to point with your toes (as when indicating an item displayed on the ground in the market) or sit with the soles of your feet pointing at other people; this is because the feet are considered to be the lowliest part of the body. When passing in front of an older person or high ranking person, especially if they are sitting down, lower your body slightly. It is polite to wait until you are given permission to eat or drink. Gracious behaviour is much appreciated by the Indonesians and will produce better results than an angry outburst.

Menstruating women and anyone with a bleeding wound must not enter temples due to a general sanction against blood on holy ground. At temple festivals, photographs without flash are fine but never stand in front of a seated priest, as one's head should not be higher than that of a holy person.

Gay and lesbian travellers

Male homosexuality is tolerated to a certain degree in traditional Balinese society, but those involved are still eventually expected to marry and have children. Flagrant displays of romance, both gay and straight, are considered very distasteful.

Green issues

Bali is suffering from acute ecological problems. The rapid and unrestrained tourist development of the island has had a massive impact on its natural environment, causing deterioration of the water quality, destruction of the coral reefs, the decline of water resources and the escalation of pollution. Hotels have been constructed without regard to the water supply and waste disposal capacity, and many commercial developments do not conform to provincial regulations regarding the protection and integrity of historical and sacred sites. Thankfully, a collective segment of Bali's hotels is setting an example through membership of Green Globe 21. There are also some recyclable-rubbish pick-up services from private households.

Health

International health certificates of vaccination against cholera and yellow fever are required only from travellers coming from infected areas. Typhoid and paratyphoid vaccinations are optional, as are Hepatitis A and B injections. Diphtheria and tetanus vaccinations are recommended. Check the following websites for updates:
World Health Organisation
www.who.int/ith/
MD Travel Health
www.mdtravelhealth.com

Kendongan fish market

Malaria and dengue fever

Malaria is not a significant problem in Bali but dengue fever is. Dengue-carrying mosquitoes are distinguished by their black-and-white banded bodies and legs and by biting in the daytime; their whine is less audible than that of other species of mosquito. They hide in dark and dank places (eg bathrooms), closets and curtains. Protect yourself with long sleeves and trousers or use a strong insect repellent *(obat anti nyamuk)*. If you are sleeping alfresco or in a non-air-conditioned room, use a mosquito net.

Minor ailments

Treat any cut or abrasion immediately, as it can easily become infected in the humid climate. Betadine, a powerful non-stinging, broad spectrum antiseptic, is available in solution or ointment at any *apotik* (pharmacy).

Sexually transmitted diseases

Gonorrhoea and herpes are on the increase in Indonesia, as are AIDS and HIV-related infections. Prostitutes are not given health check-ups, and the so-called Kuta Cowboys or local gigolos have multiple partners from all over the world. According to the chairman of an AIDS monitoring group, in 2012 the number of commercial sex workers in Bali infected with HIV/AIDS had reached 25 percent. Condoms – Indonesian and imported brands – are available at pharmacies *(apotik)*.

Bali belly

Many travellers get some form of Bali Belly at some point in their stay. Taking Lomotil and Imodium will stop the symptoms, but won't cure the infection. At the first sign of discomfort (diarrhoea and cramping), drink strong, hot tea and avoid all fruits and spicy foods. Charcoal tablets (Norit brand) will help alleviate the cramping. If you get a fever along with these symptoms, find a doctor who can prescribe antibiotics. Mineral replacement salts (Oralite brand) for dehydration should be available at every local pharmacy. Drink as much liquid as possible to avoid getting dehydrated.

Water

Bottled mineral water is widely available. All other water, including that from wells and municipal supplies, *must* be brought to a rolling boil and kept there for 10 minutes to make it safe for consumption. Iodine (Globolien) and chlorine (Halazone) tablets may also be used to make water drinkable. Brushing your teeth with untreated water is usually safe if you do not swallow the water as most toothpastes contain antibacterial substances.

Ice in eateries is generally safe, as it is manufactured at government licensed factories – but it is sometimes dumped in front of the restaurant on the dirty pavement and then only lightly washed. If in doubt, only consume drinks in cans or bottles.

Bakso (noodle soup) cart

Fruit should be peeled before eating, and avoid eating raw vegetables except at better restaurants for tourists. Go easy on spicy food if you're not used to it. It is best not to take chances with street-food vendors, but if you are dead set on it then stick to those not serving meats unless your system is already well adjusted. Remember to wash your hands thoroughly with soap.

Hospitals and clinics

Bali is getting better in terms of hygiene and medical facilities, but it still has a way to go. It is strongly recommended that you take out private health insurance before you visit. If you do need hospital treatment, particularly in the case of a life-threatening emergency, get to Singapore if your insurance policy covers medical evacuations. If not, your consulate may be able to help.

If you are in the Kuta or Nusa Dua area, BIMC (Bali International Medical Centre) and SOS Medical Clinic are geared up for the needs of tourists. For minor problems, most villages have a small government public health clinic, called *puskesmas*, used by local people and inexpensive. The luxury hotels have on-call doctors and good clinics.

Many hospitals and clinics charge different rates for Indonesians and foreigners, so check the list of fees for services to avoid getting a nasty shock when presented with the bill.

Bali International Medical Centre (BIMC)

Jl Bypass Ngurah Rai 100X, Simpang Siur, Kuta, tel: 0361-761263; www.bimc bali.com. Open 24 hours.
Kawasan BTDC Blok D, Nusa Dua, tel: 361 3000911; www.bimcbali.com. Open 24 hours.

International SOS Clinic Bali (KLINIK SOS Medika)

Jl Bypass Ngurah Rai 505X, Kuta.
24-Hour Alarm Centre: tel: 0361-710505. Clinic: tel: 0361-720100; www.sos-bali.com.

Pharmacies

If you take prescription drugs, bring a sufficient supply. Pharmacies *(apotik)* can often fill a prescription, but the dosage may not be quite the same as your doctor has prescribed. Pharmacies are widespread in the towns and tourist areas. They sell a wide range of medicines, many of which you would need a prescription for back home. Not all the assistants speak English.

Hours and holidays

Government offices in Bali are open Mon–Thur 8am–3pm, Fri 8am–noon. Banking hours are Mon–Fri 9am–3pm. Retail shops, especially in tourist areas, are open daily from 9am–9pm, but many in the cities close on Sun.

As Lombok is a Muslim island, most offices close between 11.30am and 2pm on Friday for prayers at the mosque.

At Pura Besakih, east Bali

I

Internet facilities

Internet cafés can be found all over the tourist areas of Bali; expect to pay Rp 200–500 per minute for access. At the better Internet centres, you can make use of a variety of computing services including burning CDs and downloading digital photos. Travellers with their own laptops and tablets can find wireless access at many restaurants and cafés.

L

Language

The Indonesian national tongue, Bahasa Indonesia, is spoken every-where and is written in the Roman alphabet. For some useful words and phrases, see the language chapter. Bali also has its own indigenous lan-guage, Bahasa Bali. English is spoken in the main tourist areas, and many local guides are proficient in Japanese, Russian and European languages.

M

Maps

Free maps of the island are available at many Balinese travel agencies. Most bookstores also stock maps of Bali. Useful publications are the Periplus Travel Maps of Bali (and also of Lombok and Sumbawa) and the Periplus Street Atlas Bali.

Media

Most large hotels and department stores have small bookstores, usually filled with the same tourist publica-tions, coffee-table books, novels and English-language newspapers. There are newspaper boys on the street eager to sell you newspapers from Australia and elsewhere; remember that prices are negotiable. Some local English-lan-guage newspapers are also printed daily, such as *The Jakarta Post*, *Her-ald Tribune* and *Asian Wall Street Jour-nal*, available at all major hotels, most bookstores and the magazine kiosks in Sanur, Kuta, Denpasar and Ubud. *Time*, *Newsweek* and *International Her-ald Tribune* are also available at these places. Several free tourism-oriented magazines, such as *Bali Now, Hello Bali* and *The Beat,* can be found at hotels, restaurants and visitor information cen-tres. Periplus Publishers' bookstores are widely located and found in most of the malls, offering a good selection of books on Indonesian travel, history, pol-itics and culture.

Money

The Indonesian monetary unit is the rupiah (Rp). Coins are in Rp 100, 200, 500 and 1,000 denomina-tions. Paper currency is printed for Rp 1,000, 2,000, 5,000, 10,000, 20,000, 50,000 and 100,000 notes. Be aware that there are two different versions of the Rp 10,000 note.

Participants in a temple festival

Change for high-value notes is often unavailable in smaller shops, stalls or taxis, so hang on to coins or paper currency of Rp 20,000 and below, especially when travelling in outlying areas. For safety, don't exchange large sums of money all at once if you plan to be in Indonesia for a long time.

Changing money

Foreign currency, in banknotes and traveller's cheques, is best exchanged at major banks or authorised money-changers. The best rates are in Kuta and Seminyak; Ubud rates are slightly lower. It is possible to change money in upmarket hotels but you will find that hotels and airport exchange bureaux generally give rates far below the official exchange rate.

Bring only new and crisp paper currency, especially US dollar bills, as many places will not accept old and faded ones. Smaller US dollar denominations and traveller's cheques usually get a slightly lower exchange rate. Traveller's cheques are accepted at all major hotels and at some shops. Ensure you bring your passport for identity and signature verification.

If you choose to deal with a money-changer, be extremely careful: they are renowned for their quick fingers and rigged calculators. Beware of ones who offer a higher rate as this is merely a ploy to attract your custom; only use an authorised money-changer. Make sure you get a receipt for your trans-action, and hang on to it. Reputable money-changers are 'Kuta Central' and 'BMC'. Rupiah may be converted back into foreign currency at the airport when leaving the country. Note that everyone leaving Indonesia from Ngurah Rai International Airport is required to pay an airport tax of Rp 150,000.

Credit cards

Many large shops accept major credit cards, but an additional 3–5 percent will be added to your bill. Few places outside the major hotels and big restaurants accept American Express on account of its higher commission charges.

Cash advances

Cash advances can be obtained in all the major tourist resorts and automatic teller (cash) machines (ATMs) are commonplace, especially at shopping centres and bank branches, in cities and tourist areas, but you won't find them in Amed, the Menjangan area, or in out-of-the-way rural areas.

Post

Post offices (*kantor pos*) in major towns open Mon–Thur 8am–2pm, Fri 8am–noon, Sat 8am–1pm and sometimes (eg in Ubud) Sun 8am–noon. The central post office in Denpasar, Jl Raya Niti Mandala, Renon, is open Mon–Fri 8am–8pm. Post boxes are yellow.

Temple festival at Pura Silayukti

R

Religion

Nearly 88 percent of the population in Bali is Hindu; the others are Muslim, Catholic, Protestant and Buddhist.

T

Taxes and tipping

Most hotels and restaurants add at least a 10 percent government tax on to your bill, with many high-end places charging up to a whopping 21 percent for tax and service. Tips for attentive service are appreciated in places without a service charge. If you hire a car and like the driver, then a tip of 10–15 percent is appreciated. Always carry small banknotes with you, as taxi drivers are often short of change, or so they claim. Rounding up the fare to the nearest Rp 10,000 is standard. An airport or hotel porter expects at least Rp 5,000 per bag, depending on its size and weight.

Telephones

Telephone area codes

If calling from within the same region, no area code is needed unless you are using a mobile phone. If calling from abroad, omit the initial zero. The country code for Indonesia is **62**.

Area codes are as follows:
Denpasar, Kuta, Sanur, Nusa Dua, Ubud, Gianyar, Tabanan: 0361

Singaraja, Lovina, Buleleng: 0362
Karangasem, Amlapura, Candidasa, Buitan, Amed: 0363
Negara, Jembrana: 0365
Bangli, Kintamani, Batur, Klungkung: 0366
Bedugul, Bratan: 0368
Lombok: 0370

Mobile (cell) phones

Mobile phones, which are known as handphones in Indonesia, can be used in Bali, as long as your phone operates on the GSM network. Alternatively, you can purchase a prepaid phone card and local number for around Rp 50,000. The reception quality for mobiles is generally good.

Time zones

Bali follows Central Indonesian Standard Time, eight hours ahead of Greenwich Mean Time. It is one hour ahead of Java, and in the same time zone as Singapore.

Toilets

There are few public toilets in Bali, and those that exist are generally dirty and unpleasant. Better maintained public toilets can occasionally be found at the site of tourist attractions, where you will be expected to make a nominal payment of around Rp 1000 per visit. Alternatively, if you're prepared to pay for a drink, you will always be able to use the toilet in a restaurant or *warung*. Expect squat toilets and no toilet paper in the simple *warungs*.

Taman Tirtagangga water park

Tourist information

Denpasar (Ngurah Rai International) Airport: tel: 0361-751011.
Denpasar Government Tourism Office: Jl Surapati 7, Denpasar; tel: 0361-234569.
Badung Tourism Office: Jl S.Parman, Renon; tel: 0361-222387.
Bali Tourism Board: Jl Raya Puputan, Niti Mandala, Denpasar; tel: 0361-239200.
Bali Tourist Information Centre: Jl Bunisari 7, Kuta; tel: 0361-753530.
Bina Wisata Ubud Tourist Office: Jl Raya Ubud; tel: 0361-973285; 8am–8pm.

Transport

Airport and arrival

The domestic departures and international terminals at the airport are within walking distance of each other.
Denpasar Airport (also known as Ngurah Rai International Airport): tel: 0361-751025/0361-751011; Customs tel: 0361-756714; www.ngurahrai-airport.co.id. Office hours: Mon–Thur 8am–4.30pm, Fri 8am–3.30pm.

Distances from the airport are as follows: Kuta 4km (2.5miles), Legian 6km (4 miles), Seminyak 9km (6 miles), Kerobokan 14km (9 miles), Canggu 20km (12 miles), Nusa Dua 13km (8 miles), Jimbaran 6km (4 miles), Ubud 39km (24 miles) and Lovina 92km (57 miles). Be warned that traffic jams are commonplace.

If you have not made prior arrangements with your hotel to pick you up, there is a taxi service from the airport in Bali that you can use; fixed rates to various destinations are posted at the counter. Pay the cashier at the desk and receive a coupon that is to be handed over to your driver, who will be summoned for you.

The only forms of public transport from the airport are taxis and hotel pick-up services.

Public transport
Minivans

Minivans *(bemo)* operate on fixed routes from terminals or marketplaces in cities and major towns. Some transfer points are at important crossroads. There are no marked places to get off and on; just flag them down and call out 'stop' when you want to get out. Fares are based on distance travelled and always very cheap, at just a few thousand rupiah. Always carry small change with you; you can't expect a *bemo* driver to give you change from a Rp 50,000, or even a Rp 20,000, banknote.

As passengers and products, and even live chickens, get loaded off and on, vans can get hot and crowded. This mode of transport does take time but allows you to meet local people; beware of pickpockets, though.

Buses

Major bus terminals are at Tegal in Denpasar (services to Kuta); Kereneng in Denpasar (services to destinations

Fishing boats on Lake Bratan

within the city, Batubulan and Sanur); Ubung (services to Tabanan, Singaraja and Jembrana); and Batubulan (services to Gianyar, Singaraja, Bangli, Klungkung and Karangasem). A new Trans Sarbagita government bus service has been operating in South Bali since 2011. The buses are comfortable and air-conditioned and the fixed fare is only Rp 3,500. These buses stop only at permanent elevated bus stops built on the road curb.

Shuttle services

Shuttle services operate daily between Kuta, Ubud, Sanur, Lovina and Candidasa. Although they cost a bit more than buses or *bemo,* they are faster and more comfortable. Tickets are available from most hotels and tourist agencies.

Private transport

Taxis

Taxis are metered or have fixed rates from the airport to the major hotels. Check with the driver before you board the taxi, as many drivers prefer to charge a flat rate instead of using the meter. Ask your hotel concierge what the going rate is for the destination you want to get to. Few taxis, outside of the Kuta-Legian-Seminyak area, cruise the streets for passengers, so you need to call up (or ask your hotel concierge to call a taxi for you). The best company is Bali Taxi (Bluebird Group), the light blue cabs, with a reputation for being clean, reliable, safe and honest. Most drivers speak English, especially the drivers of Bali Taxi cabs.

Bali Taxi, tel: 0361-701111 (complaints tel: 0361-701621)

There are very few taxis in Ubud; the only ones you will see are those that have brought passengers from other tourist areas and are hoping for a fare back. You can arrange private transport with your hotel or negotiate a fare with one of the many young men offering transport on the street.

Motorcycle taxis

Young men operate motorcycle taxis known as *ojek,* which can be very convenient for locations not serviced by public transport. Agree on the price beforehand, and make sure you wear the extra helmet that the driver provides, as it's required by law. The drivers do weave in and out of heavy traffic but are very experienced. Fares are usually just a few thousand rupiah for a short journey and no more than about half of what you would pay for a taxi.

Vehicle with driver

Chartering a car or minivan with driver can be done by the half-day or full-day. Rates are cheaper if negotiated on the street rather than from your hotel; look out for young men who call out 'transpor' and move their hands as if driving a car. The amount should include fuel. Daily rates are generally between Rp 300,000 and Rp 500,000. Alternatively you can rent a car and pay about Rp 100,000 extra per day for the services of an English-speaking driver.

Driving through Jatiluwih

Car and motorcycle hire

Driving in Bali can be dangerous. Generally, drivers do not drive defensively, the roads are narrow and poorly maintained, and stray dogs and chickens frequently dart into the road. If you collide with anything, you are responsible for all costs. It's safer to hire a driver while you relax and enjoy the sights. Driving is on the left-hand side of the road in Bali.

Motorcycles are a convenient and inexpensive way to get around the island, but there are risks due to heavy traffic and poor roads. Helmets are required by law, but the cheap ones provided by rental agencies offer little protection, so bring your own or buy a good one from a local shop, especially one with a face shield for protection from sun, rain, bugs and dust. Drive slowly and defensively, as locals and tourists are injured or killed every year in accidents.

The cost of motorbike hire varies according to the model, condition of the machine, length of rental, and time of the year. Around Rp 80,000 to Rp 100,000 per day is usual. Petrol is not included. Buy full insurance so that you are covered for any damage. Be sure to test drive your bike, to check that everything is in working order, especially brakes and lights. Most rental bikes are 125cc or smaller, although larger bikes are available.

You should have an international driving permit valid for motorcycles, or else go to the Denpasar Police Office to obtain a temporary permit, valid for three months on Bali only. Normally the person who rents you the motorbike will accompany you to the police office. Bring your passport, driving licence from your home country, and three passport-sized photographs.

Visas and passports

The following information is accurate at time of press, but subject to change at any time.

If you have a British, US, Canadian, Australian or New Zealand passport, you are eligible for visa-on-arrival (VOA) when visiting Bali and Indonesia; this costs US$25 for 30 days. This also applies to travellers from most European countries. Processing is relatively fast, 3–5 minutes per applicant, and those who cannot pay in US dollars can change money on the spot.

Your passport must be valid for at least six months from the date of entry into Indonesia, you must have proof of onward passage (either return or through tickets), and you must complete a disembarkation document.

Weights and measures

Indonesia uses the metric system. Temperatures are measured in degrees Celsius.

Gianyar food market signs

LANGUAGE

Bahasa Indonesia

The English language is widely spoken in all tourist areas of Bali, and many local guides are trained in Japanese and the major European languages.

Although more than 350 languages and dialects are spoken in the archipelago, the Indonesian language and national tongue, known as Bahasa Indonesia, is spoken everywhere and easy to learn. Derived from Old Malay, which was for centuries the trading language of the Indies, it was first embraced in 1928 by the nationalist movement as the "language of national unity", a political tool to bring the diverse religious and ethnic groups of the archipelago together. Bahasa Indonesia is also the official language, used in commerce, schools and the media.

Bahasa Indonesia is a non-tonal language and written in the Roman alphabet. It is among the easiest of all spoken languages to learn as there are no tenses, plurals or genders, and often just one word can convey the meaning of a whole sentence.

There are a few basic rules of grammar in Bahasa Indonesia. To indicate the past, prefix the verb with *sudah* (already). For the future, prefix the verb with *belum* (not yet) or *akan* (will). The word *pergi*, for example, is used to say that you are going, you went, and you have gone. The word *makan* is used to say that you are eating, you ate, and you have eaten. *Saya sudah makan* means 'I already ate'; *saya belum makan* means 'I've not yet eaten'; *saya akan pergi* means 'I will go'. To make a noun plural, the word is usually just repeated, e.g. *anak* (child), *anak anak* (children).

Spelling is phonetic with a few twists: The letter 'c' is pronounced 'ch' (eg. *Candidasa*, *Canggu*); the letter 'g' is always hard (eg. *gamelan*, Garuda); 'y' is pronounced 'j' (eg. Yogyakarta); the letter 'c' is sometimes spelled 'tj' (eg. Tjampuhan instead of Campuhan); the letter 'j' can also be spelled 'dj' (eg. Djakarta instead of Jakarta); and there is no letter 'v': November, for example, is spelt Nopember.

Indonesians always show respect when addressing others, especially their elders. The custom is to address an older man as *bapak* or *mas* (Mr) and an older woman as *ibu* (Madam/Mrs).

General terms

Hello *Halo*
How are you? *Apa kabar?*
Fine, thanks *Baik, terima kasih*
Good morning *Selamat pagi*
Good afternoon *Selamat siang*
Good evening *Selamat malam*
Goodbye *Selamat tinggal*
Please *Tolong*

Selling fruit in Denpasar

Thank you Terima kasih
You're welcome Sama-sama
Yes Ya
No Tidak
Excuse me (to get past) Permisi
I'm sorry maafkan saya
I'd like... Saya mau...
How much? Berapa harganya?
Where is...? ...di mana?
I don't understand Saya tidak mengerti
Can you repeat that? Bisa diulangi?
Do you speak English? Apakah anda bias berbicara dalam bahasa Inggris?
I don't speak Indonesian Saya tidak bias bicara bahasa Indonesia
Where's the restroom? Kamar kecil di mana?
What's your name? Siapa nama anda?
My name is... nama saya...
Where are you from? Anda dari mana?
I'm from the US/UK Saya dari Amerika/Inggris
Please help me Tolonglah saya

Food and drink

restaurant restoran
A table for..., please Tolong meja untuk...
Can we sit...? Bisa kami duduk...?
here/there di sini/di sana
outside di luar
in a non-smoking area di area tidak merokok
The check (bill), please Tolong minta bonnya
Is service included? Apakah sudah termasuk pelayanan?

Is it spicy? Apakah pedas?
I'm vegetarian Saya vegetarian
What's this? Apa ini?
Coffee/tea... kopi/the...
...with milk pakai susu
...with sugar pakai gula
(sparkling/still) water air (sparkling/still)
Beef sapi
Chicken ayam
Duck bebek
Lamb kambing
Pork babi
Steak steak
Veal anak sapi
Rice beras
Noodles mie
Potato kentang
Tofu tahu
Vegetable sayuran
Egg telur
Fish ikan
Pepper (chilli) cabai

Internet

Can I access the internet/check email here? Burada internete girebilir/postalarimi kontrol edebilir miyim?
How much per hour/half hour? Saati/Yarim saati ne kadar?
Does it have wireless internet? Kablosuz internet var mi?
What is the WiFi password? Kablosuz agin sifresi nedir?
Is the WiFi free? Apakah WiFi-nya gratis?
Are you on Facebook/Twitter? Facebook/Twitter'da misin?

BOOKS AND FILM

If you are interested in delving deeper into Bali and aspects of Balinese culture, try one of the following books or films.

History and culture

Bali: Sekala & Niskala Volume I – Essays on Religion, Ritual and Art, by Fred B. Eiseman. An exploration of Balinese religion, ritual and performing arts.

Bali Sekala and Niskala Volume II – Essays on Society, Tradition and Craft, by Fred B. Eiseman. Covers the geography, social organisation, language, folklore and material culture of Bali.

A Short History of Bali, by Robert Pringle. The history of Bali from before the Bronze Age to the presidency of Megawati Sukarnoputri and the tragedy of the Kuta bombings in 2002.

Bali: A Paradise Created, by Adrian Vickers. Bali, the "last Paradise", seen through Western eyes. Fresh insights on the history and culture of a traditional island faced with a massive invasion of paradise-seekers.

Fiction

A Tale from Bali, by Vicki Baum. First published in 1937, this wonderful and classic tale of love and death in Bali is set against the backdrop of turmoil faced by the Balinese in their struggle against the Dutch colonialists.

A Little Bit One O'clock, by William Ingram. A beautifully written novel exploring the web of relationships within a Balinese family.

Midnight Shadows, by Garrett Kam. Historical novel with the Communist coup of 1965 as the setting. It looks at the reasons behind the terrible violence that engulfed the island by interweaving actual events and history with mythology, dreams and rituals.

The Year of Living Dangerously, by C.J. Koch. Banned in Indonesia for many years and later made into a film, this is the tale of a nation in crisis during the overthrow of President Sukarno. Masterfully told.

Art/music/dance

Offerings, the Ritual Art of Bali, by Francine Brinkgreve and David Stuart-Fox. This beautifully illustrated book provides a rare glimpse into the pageantry, ritual and devotion that accompany the creation of offerings in Bali.

Dance and Drama in Bali, by Beryl de Zoete and Walter Spies. This important ethnographical book documents the history of Balinese dance and drama. Spies lived in Bali for 12 years from 1927 and was an accomplished painter, musician and dance expert.

Shadow puppets for sale in Sukawati village

De Zoete was trained in European dance.

Balinese Paintings (second edition), by A.A.M. Djelantik. A concise but well-documented guide to traditional Balinese paintings, including that of Ubud's Pita-maha painters and the Young Artists of Batuan and Penestanan.

Bali Sacred and Secret, by Gill Marais. A remarkable revelation of a rarely-witnessed, mystical world of Balinese ritual and magic.

A House in Bali, by Colin McPhee. First published in 1947 and one of the most enchanting books ever written about Bali, this book tells the story of how, in 1929, a young Canadian-born musician chanced upon rare gramophone recordings of Balinese gamelan music that were to change his life forever.

General

Secrets of Bali, by Jonathan Copeland with Ni Wayan Murni. From Balinese gods to Balinese *gamelan*, difficult subjects are simply explained in this beautifully written and illustrated work.

Bali Today – Real Balinese Stories, by Jean Couteau. Couteau is well known for his humorous stories in the Indonesian press about Bali and the Balinese way of life. His observations are witty, ingenious and hilariously funny.

The Island of Bali, by Miguel Covarrubias. First published in 1937, this book is still regarded by many as the most authoritative text on Bali and its culture and people.

Eat, Pray, Love, by Elizabeth Gilbert. Traces the author's journey through Italy, India and Bali on a quest to discover worldly pleasure, spiritual devotion, and what she really wants out of life. Look out for the Hollywood film starring Julia Roberts and Javier Bardem, which is partly filmed on location in Bali.

Our Hotel in Bali, by Louise G. Koke. A re-issue of the 1987 publication that documents how a young American couple, Bob Koke and Louise Garret, came to build Bali's first hotel in 1936, the Kuta Beach Hotel.

Dragons in the Bath, by Cat Wheeler. A Canadian writer retires to a country town in Bali and learns to deal with randy ducks, rampant vegetation, roasted spiders, a haunted river bank and all the quirks and delights of living in a Balinese community.

Film

The island of Belitung, off the coast of Sumatra, is known for Tanjung Tinggi beach and its extraordinary rock formations. The enormously successful Indonesian film *Laskar Pelangi* (Rainbow Troops) was shot here, and the film's amazing beach scenes have made it a popular holiday destination among locals. *The Act of Killing*, a critically acclaimed documentary released in 2013, involves former Indonesian death squad leaders re-enacting the murders they committed. The killings of 1965–66 were part of an anti-Communist movement.

ABOUT THIS BOOK

This *Explore Guide* has been produced by the editors of Insight Guides, whose books have set the standard for visual travel guides since 1970. With top-quality photography and authoritative recommendations, these guidebooks bring you the very best routes and itineraries in the world's most exciting destinations.

BEST ROUTES

The routes in the book provide something to suit all budgets, tastes and trip lengths. As well as covering the destination's many classic attractions, the itineraries track lesser-known sights and areas away from the main urban and tourist hubs. The routes embrace a range of interests, so whether you are an art fan, a gourmet, a history buff or have kids to entertain, you will find an option to suit.

We recommend reading the whole of a route before setting out. This should help you to familiarise yourself with it and enable you to plan where to stop for refreshments – options are shown in the 'Food and Drink' box at the end of each tour.

For our pick of the tours by theme, consult Recommended Routes for… (see pages 4–5).

INTRODUCTION

The routes are set in context by this introductory section, giving an overview of the destination to set the scene, plus background information on food and drink, shopping and more, while a succinct history timeline highlights the key events over the centuries.

DIRECTORY

Also supporting the routes is a Directory chapter, with a clearly organised A–Z of practical information, our pick of where to stay while you are there and select restaurant listings; these eateries complement the more low-key cafés and restaurants that feature within the routes and are intended to offer a wider choice for evening dining. Also included here are some nightlife listings, plus a handy language guide and our recommendations for books and films about the destination.

ABOUT THE AUTHORS

Born and raised in England, Rachel Lovelock's childhood dream was to become a writer and live on a tropical island, but she followed the advice of her careers teacher and worked for a UK-based corporate company instead. She finally realised her dream when she moved to Bali on a whim in 1998. She fell in love with the island and has been living there ever since, writing prolifically for magazines, guidebooks and websites. Her work covers a variety of topics, ranging from culture, tourist destinations and activities, to restaurants and luxury villas. You can read about her travels and adventures on her website and blog: www.indiestravelwriter.com

CONTACT THE EDITORS

We hope you find this Explore Guide useful, interesting and a pleasure to read. If you have any questions or feedback on the text, pictures or maps, please do let us know. If you have noticed any errors or outdated facts, or have suggestions for places to include on the routes, we would be delighted to hear from you. Please drop us an email at insight@apaguide.co.uk. Thanks!

CREDITS

Explore Bali
Contributors: Rachel Lovelock
Commissioning Editor: Catherine Dreghorn
Series Editor: Sarah Clark
Pictures/Art: Tom Smyth/Shahid Mahmood
Map Production: Berndston and Berndston GmbH, updated by Apa Cartography Department
Production: Tynan Dean and Rebeka Davies

Photo credits: Alamy 4/5T, 50, 50/51, 51L, 56; Anon 70/71; AWL Images 42/43; Corrie Wingate/Apa Publications 0/1, 2ML, 2MC, 2MR, 2MR, 2MC, 2ML, 2/3T, 4TL, 4MC, 4ML, 4BC, 5MR, 4/5M, 6ML, 6MC, 6ML, 6MC, 6MR, 6MR, 6/7T, 8T, 8B, 8/9, 9L, 10, 12, 12/13, 13L, 14T, 14B, 14/15, 16T, 16B, 16/17, 17L, 18T, 18B, 18/19, 20, 20/21, 22, 24, 26ML, 26MC, 26MR, 26ML, 26MC, 26MR, 26/27T, 28, 28/29, 30, 30/31, 31L, 32L, 32/33, 33, 34, 34/35, 37L, 36/37, 38, 38/39, 40, 40/41, 41L, 44, 44/45, 46, 46/47, 47L, 48, 48/49, 49L, 52, 52/53, 54, 54/55, 55L, 56/57, 58, 58/59, 59L, 60, 60/61, 62, 62/63, 64, 65L, 66, 66/67, 68, 68/69, 69L, 72, 72/73, 74, 74/75, 75L, 76, 76/77, 78, 79L, 78/79, 80, 80/81, 81L, 82ML, 82MC, 82MR, 82MR, 82MC, 82ML, 82/83T, 84, 84/85, 85L, 86, 86/87, 92, 94, 94/95, 96, 96/97, 98, 98/99, 100, 100/101, 101L, 102, 102/103, 103L, 104/105, 106, 106/107, 110, 110/111, 112, 112/113, 114, 114/115, 116, 116/117, 118, 118/119, 120/121; Dreamstime 5MR, 22/23, 88, 88/89, 90, 90/91, 92/93, 104; Getty Images 24/25; iStockphoto.com 11L, 10/11; Jack Hollingsworth/Apa Publications 64/65; Kevin Jones/Apa Publications 36, 39L, 108/109; Tips 70
Cover credits: Main: Temple procession with colorful offerings, Getty; Front Cover BL: JL Sulawesi, Fabric shop, Corrie Wingate/Apa Publications; Back Cover: (Left) Belimbing rice terraces; (Right): Seaweed farmer houses, near Jungutbatu Bay, Corrie Wingate/Apa Publications

Printed by CTPS – China
© 2014 Apa Publications (UK) Ltd
All Rights Reserved

First Edition 2014

DISTRIBUTION

Worldwide
APA Publications GmbH & Co. Verlag KG (Singapore branch)
7030 Ang Mo Kio Ave 5, 08-65
Northstar @ AMK, Singapore 569880
Email: apasin@singnet.com.sg
UK and Ireland
Dorling Kindersley Ltd (a Penguin Company)
80 Strand, London, WC2R 0RL, UK
Email: sales@uk.dk.com
US
Ingram Publisher Services
One Ingram Blvd, PO Box 3006, La Vergne, TN 37086-1986
Email: ips@ingramcontent.com
Australia
Universal Publishers
PO Box 307, St. Leonards NSW 1590
Email: sales@universalpublishers.com.au
New Zealand
Brown Knows Publications
11 Artesia Close, Shamrock Park, Auckland, New Zealand 2016
Email: sales@brownknows.co.nz

INDEX

A

Air Panas hot springs **68**
Amed **60**
Amlapura **59**
    Puri Kanginan (palace) **59**
Asahduren **71**

B

Bangkiansidem **37**
Bangli **52**
bartering **18**
Batur Volcano Museum, Penelokan **42**
Bedulu **45, 51**
Belayu **75**
Belimbing **71**
bird-watching **22**
books **120**
Brahma Arama Vihara (monastery) **68**
Bukit Demulih **52**
Bukit Peninsula **32**
    Pura Luhur Uluwatu **32**
    Uluwatu Beach **34**
Bunut Bolong **72**

C

Campuhan **37**
Candidasa **56**
Ceking **48**
children **106**
climate **10**

D

Danau Batur (lake) **43**
Danau Buyan **64**
Danau Tamblingan **64**
dance **20**
Denpasar **30**
    Catur Muka **31**
    Jl Hasanudin **31**
    Jl Sulawesi **31**
    Museum Bali **30**
    Pasar Badung **31**
    Pasar Kumbasari **31**
    Puputan Square **31**
    Pura Jagatnatha **30**
disabled travellers **107**
dolphin-watching **67**

E

economy **12**
Elephant Safari Park **49**
emergencies **108**

F

festivals **20**
film **121**
food and drink **14**

G

geography **8**
Goa Gajah **45**
golf **23**
Gunung Agung **54**
Gunung Batukau **73**
    Pura Luhur Batukau (temple) **76**
Gunung Batur volcano **42, 43**

H

health **109**
history **24**
horse riding **23**
Hotels
    Adirama **92**
    Alila Manggis **91**
    Amankila Resort **91**
    Amarta **92**
    Ayana Resort and Spa **87**
    Bali Hyatt **89**
    Bali Paradise Hotel **92**
    Bulgari Resort **88**
    Casa Padma Suites **85**
    Cempaka Belimbing Villas **93**
    Conrad Bali **89**
    Damai Lovina Villas **93**
    Dhyana Pura Beach Resort **86**
    Elephant Safari Park Lodge **93**
    Four Seasons Resort **88**
    Four Seasons Sayan **90**
    Gajah Mina Beach Resort **93**
    Grand Hyatt Bali **90**
    Hai Tide Huts **92**
    Hard Rock Hotel **86**
    Hotel Kumala Pantai **86**
    Hotel Sanur Beach **89**
    Hotel Tugu Bali **87**
    Karma Kandara **88**
    Lakeview Restaurant & Hotel **91**
    La Taverna Hotel **89**
    Mystique Apartments **87**
    Nikko Bali Resort **90**
    Pacung Mountain Resort **93**
    Padma Resort Bali at Legian **86**
    Pelangi Bali Hotel **87**
    Poppies Cottages I **86**
    Rocky Bungalows **89**
    Tandjung Sari Hotel **89**
    Tegal Sari **90**
    The Beverly Hills **88**
    The Legian **87**
    The Oberoi **87**
    The Watergarden **92**
    Ubud Hanging Gardens **91**
    Ubud Village Hotel **91**
    Ulun Ubud **91**
    Un's Hotel **86**

J

Jatiluwih **75**
Jimbaran Bay **34**

K

Kalibukbuk **67**
Kedewatan **37**

Kintamani **42**
Klungkung **53**
    Bale Kembang **53**
    Kerta Gosa **53**
    Puputan Klungkung
        Monument **54**
Kota Gianyar **52**
Krambitan **70**
Kuta **32**
Kutri **52**

L

Lake Bratan **61**
    Bali Treetop Adventure
        Park **63**
    Candikuning **61**
    Kebun Eka Raya
        Botanical Gardens
        63
    Pura Ulun Danu Bratan
        (temple) **62**
    Taman Rekreasi Bedugul
        63
language **118**
local customs **10**
Lovina **66**

M

Medewi **72**
Menjangan Island **69**
money **112**
mountain cycling **23**
Muncan **55**
Munduk **64**
Munduk Waterfall **65**
Museum Puri Lukisan **39**

N

Neka Art Museum **38**
nightlife **104**
Nusa Ceningan **80**
Nusa Lembongan **77**
    Devil's Tear **78**
    Jungut Batu **78**
    Lembongan village **78**
    Rumah di Bawah Tanah

79
Nusa Penida **80**
    Goa Karangsari **81**
    Pura Dalem Ped (temple)
        80
    Sebuluh Waterfall **81**
    Toyopakeh **80**

P

Pacung **75**
paragliding **23**
Pejeng **50**
    Museum Prbakala
        Gedong Arca **51**
    Pura Kebo Edan (temple)
        51
    Pura Panataran Sasih
        (temple) **50**
    Pura Pusering Jagat
        (temple) **50**
Pemuteran **69**
Petulu **40**
politics **12**
population **10**
Pura Alas Kedaton (temple)
    74
Pura Besakih (temple) **54**
Pura Gunung Kawi (temple)
    47
Pura Gunung Lebah
    (temple) **38**
Pura Kehen (temple) **52**
Pura Mengening (temple)
    48
Pura Pengukur-ukuran
    (temple) **47**
Pura Puncak Payogan
    (temple) **37**
Pura Puncak Penulisan
    (temple) **44**
Pura Samuan Tiga (temple)
    46
Pura Tanah Lot (temple) **74**
Pura Tirtha Empul **48**
Pura Ulun Danu Batur
    (temple) **44**

R

Restaurants
    Adirama **103**
    Barberkyu Kafe **100**
    Bebek Bengil (Dirty Duck)
        100
    Bumbu Bali **100**
    Cafe Batujimbar **95**
    Cafe Belimbing **72**
    Cafe des Artistes **100**
    Cafe Lotus **41**
    Cafe Made **69**
    Cafe Pandan **81**
    Cafe Teras **65**
    Candi Agung **102**
    Casa Luna **101**
    Danau Toba **96**
    Elephant Park Restaurant
        102
    ExtraBlatt **96**
    Garpu **102**
    Gateway of India **97**
    Hongkong **34**
    Ibu Oka **101**
    Indus **41**
    Jamsine Kitchen **103**
    Jojo's Restaurant **81**
    Kafe Batan Waru **41**
    Kakatua Bar &
        Restaurant **69**
    Kampung Cafe **49**
    Khi Khi Seafood
        Restaurant **103**
    Kori Restaurant & Bar
        96
    Ku De Ta **98**
    Kunyit Bali **96**
    Lakeview Hotel **101**
    La Lucciola Restaurant &
        Bar **98**
    Lamak **102**
    La Rouge **60**
    La Sal **98**
    Lereng Agung Restoran
        55
    Lihat Sawah **102**

Made's Warung 97
Ma Joly 97
Mama San 98
Mangrove Stop
    Restaurant 81
Massimo il Ristorante
    95
Menega Cafe 34
Metis 98
Mezzanine Restaurant &
    Bar 95
Mozaic 101
Mykonos Taverna 98
Naga Restaurant 103
Nampu 100
Naughty Nuri's 41
Ngiring Ngewedang 65
Nyoman Mawa 102
Pacung Indah Hotel &
    Restaurant 76
Plantations 103
Poppies Restaurant 97
Rasa Sayang 96
Rosso Vivo 97
Sanur Beach Market 95
Sardine 99
Sarong 99
Sate Bali 99
Stiff Chilli 95
Strawberry Stop 65

Sunda Kelapa 34
Sundara 99
Taco Beach 99
Terazo 41
The Beach House 76
The Italian Restaurant
    100
The Junction 97
The Restaurant at Damai
    Villas 65
TJ's Mexican Restaurant
    97
Trattoria 99
Tut Mak 101
Vincent's 60
Warung Aria 103
Watergarden Kafe 60

S
Sacred Monkey Forest 39
Sanda 71
Sanur 28
    Bali Hyatt 28
    Museum Le Mayeur 29
    Taman Werdhi Budaya
        Art Centre 30
Seminyak 32
shopping 18
Sidemen 55
Singaraja 67

Gedong Kertya 68

T
Taman Ujung 59
Tampaksiring 47
Tegallalang 49
Tenganan 56
Tirtagangga 60
tourism 9
Toya Bungkah 43
transport 115
trekking 23
Trunyan 44

U
Ubud 35
    Pura Taman Sariswati
        36
    Puri Saren (royal palace)
        36
    Ubud Market 35

W
water sports 22
West Bali National Park 69
white-water rafting 23

Y
Yeh Panas hot springs 76
Yeh Pulu 51

MAP LEGEND

● Start of tour	♠ Balinese temple
→ Tour & route direction	♀ ψ Buddhist/Hindu temple
❶ Recommended sight	✉ Main post office
❷ Recommended restaurant/café	🚌 Main bus station
★ Place of interest	∴ Ancient Site
❶ Tourist information	--- Ferry route
⚊ Statue/monument	● National park
	◖ Cave / volcano
	Waterfall / reef

- - - Regional boundary

Park

Important building

Hotel

Transport hub

Shopping / market

Pedestrian area

Urban area

INSIGHT GUIDES

INSPIRING YOUR NEXT ADVENTURE

Insight Guides offers you a range of travel guides
to match your needs. Whether you are looking for
inspiration for planning a trip, cultural information,
walks and tours, great listings, or practical advice, we
have a product to suit you.